NO
How to welcome people
DISABLED
with disabilities into your life
SOULS
and your church

D1456825

JIM PIERSON

STANDARD PUBLISHING

Cincinnati, Ohio

Library of Congress Cataloging-in-Publication Data

Pierson, Jim
    No disabled souls : how to welcome people with disabilities into your life and your church / Jim Pierson.
        p.   cm.
    Includes bibliographical references.
    ISBN 0-7847-0768-5
    1. Handicapped. 2. Friendship. 3. Social acceptance. 4. Helping behavior. 5. Church work with the handicapped. I. Title.
    HV1568.P54   1998
    302.3'4'087—dc21   98-9994
                                                                                         CIP

Edited by Theresa C. Hayes
Cover design by Matt Key
Illustrations (including cover) by Rodney Pate

The Standard Publishing Company, Cincinnati, Ohio
A division of Standex International Corporation

05   04   03   02   01   00   99   98   5   4   3   2   1

NO
DISABLED
SOULS

APPRECIATION

After writing this book, my gratitude to several organizations and people became apparent.

THE ORGANIZATIONS

The East Tennessee Children's Rehabilitation Center, which I directed from 1967-1984, provided a foundation for my professional life in the disability world.

Johnson Bible College has offered unique opportunities for me to develop courses and a minor (the first of its kind) in disability ministry. I am grateful to President David Eubanks and Academic Dean Richard Beam. It has been a thirty-eight-year blessing.

Standard Publishing has increased my field of professional involvement. Doing workshops for Christian education meetings, assisting in the production of disability ministry materials, and helping guide the company's philosophy have broadened my experience. Dr. Eugene Wigginton, Standard's president, summarizes the philosophy, "It's more than the law, it's love." I am grateful to Gene, his predecessors, and his successor, Mark Taylor.

The board of directors of The Christian Church Foundation for the Handicapped who have given me the opportunity to develop a ministry from scratch. With their confidence, goodwill, financial support, prayers, and friendship, they have allowed me to be creative in an atmosphere of freedom. I am especially grateful to Dr. Sam Stone and Dr. Jack Ballard, the two chairmen of the board in our fourteen-year history.

I am grateful to my excellent editor, Theresa Hayes, who improved the words and encouraged the author.

I am grateful to the families of the people whose stories I shared. They provided information, photographs, and encouragement.

I am grateful to my staff at the Christian Church Foundation for the Handicapped. Rachel Marsh served as computer advisor. Carolyn Proctor typed many pages of material. Judy Davis corrected the manuscript from my handwritten notes.

I am grateful to my wife, Norma, who for thirty-four years has been my best friend, my most trusted adviser, and my constant encourager.

I am grateful to Sean, my second grandchild, who has been a delight in the entire process of writing "his book."

A TIP FROM A TODDLER

His name is Sean. He has been a part of my life since December 27, 1991. Being his grandfather is one of my special blessings. Sean enjoys people, people enjoy him.

Some of my favorite memories of Sean are of when he started to talk. Whenever he saw someone he didn't know, he would ask, "What is your name?" For example, when the family was out for a meal, Sean would announce to the server, "My name is Sean. This is my brother Derek. This is my mom. This is my grandmother. What is your name?"

Sean's all-inclusive approach to strangers showed me a way to promote inclusion for those with disabilities: Ask the person what his name is!

My friends with disabilities have lots of names. They have lots of diagnoses. They are young and old. They live in several states and three or four countries. They work in sheltered workshops with their peers. They live in group homes with their peers. Whatever their situations, they need friends with disabilities and friends without disabilities.

In the three decades I've worked with people with disabilities, there have been many positive changes in their education and care. But the more than fifty-four million people with disabilities in the United States need more than an advocate; they need a friend. Inclusion, the process of making them a part of their communities, is the one change that will bring the most benefit. The task is not overwhelming. It can be accomplished one person at a time. And it will happen best and quickest when a person without a disability accepts the responsibility of forming a friendship with a person who has a disability.

People with disabilities are a part of your world. Every day they walk where you walk. You nod to the lady from a group home who attends your church. At the market you are waited on by a man with a physical disability. Your new neighbors have a child with autism. Your golfing buddy tells you his nephew has been paralyzed by a skiing accident. Respond. The important issues are not diagnosis, cause, and prognosis. Friendship is. Go out of your way to create opportunities to express friendship.

As a friend to a person with a disability, your significant role will be to help him participate in the routines of community life. In 1991, The National Organization on Disability commissioned Louis Harris and Associates to conduct the N.O.D./Harris Survey of Americans with Disabilities. The survey determined

" MY NAME IS SEAN. WHAT IS YOUR NAME?"

the progress that has been made in the levels of participation among people with and people without disabilities since a similar Harris survey in 1986. During the five-year span, the differences persisted. The study found that "only 35 percent of people with disabilities ate in a restaurant once a week or more, nearly the same percentage as in 1986, and much less than the 55 percent of the nondisabled population who do so. Barely 40 percent of Americans with disabilities had gone to a movie in the last year, up only slightly from about one-third in 1986. And about one-quarter of the respondents with disabilities in 1994 had attended a live music or sports event during the previous year—about the same proportion as eight years earlier."[1] A nondisabled friend can change those percentages.

My purposes in writing this book are to answer questions you may have about the disability community and to encourage you to develop a friendship with a person with a disability. The "how-tos" of building a friendship are important but, by far, the most important step is to see people with disabilities as people. To help you in this regard I have filled this book with stories about my friends with disabilities and their influence on my life and my world.

WANT TO *make a new friend? Ask, "What is your name?"*

When you finish this book, you will be able to befriend a person with a disability and make him or her a part of your life, your community, and your church. The process begins with Sean's question, "What is your name?"

[1]National Organization on Disability. *Closing the Gap. The N.O.D./Harris Survey of Americans With Disabilities—A Summary.* Washington, DC, 1994.

CHAPTER 1

MORE ALIKE THAN DIFFERENT

His name is Stephen. His father, Ed Smith, directed "Crossroads," a ministry to the disability community based in Brisbane, Australia. During the International Year of the Disabled Person in 1981, I was invited by Crossroads to Australia as a speaker. After a disability awareness speech at Alcorn College in Brisbane, I met Stephen.

I was walking to lunch with six other conference participants. Because of the narrow sidewalks, we had to walk in pairs. Our pairing off had left a young man with a disability without a partner. Excusing myself from my walking partner, I approached him and asked him his name.

"Stephen," he replied.

"My name is Jim," I said.

"I know," he answered, "I heard you talk."

I wanted to say to him, "And I almost didn't practice what I was preaching." Instead, I asked him if he would help me order lunch. He agreed to help me.

In the eatery, he ordered a meat pie and responded in the affirmative when asked if he wanted peas on it. I ordered the same, complete with the peas. Although Stephen and I hit it off immediately, I learned then that I don't care for peas on my meat pies!

Stephen's story had a familiar twist. After adopting him, his parents learned that he had a disability.

He was dually diagnosed with mental retardation and emotional disturbance. When I met this healthy, good-looking man in his early twenties, he worked in a sheltered workshop (a non-competitive employment situation), went to church, traveled widely, and seemed to be in touch with his environment. Because of Australia's generous pensions to its disabled citizens, Stephen seemed to have all of his needs met. He functioned well with his family. Two brothers gave him positive attention.

One evening my family and I had dinner with Stephen's family in their home in Goodna, a suburb of Brisbane. This pleasant time gave me an unexpected opportunity to observe the emotional part of my friend's diagnosis. During the eating of a typical Australian baked dinner (which included pumpkin!), some factor not obvious to me prompted an angry outburst from Stephen. Quickly his parents got him out of the dining room. Following a quiet conversation with them, he returned to the table. The nice evening of international friendship continued.

Each of us is a heartbeat away from a stroke, an automobile accident, or a fall that could leave us with a disability.

When I learned that Stephen would be a part of a two-week trip to Australia's famous outback, I recalled the incident and wondered if the pressures of travel, different schedules, and new people would produce similar reactions. My family and I were participants in this trip, which was part of Crossroads' travel program. On a trip like this one, half of the group were enablers and the other half persons with disabilities. The "able-bodied" group assisted the ones with disabilities. For example, I assisted a man who could have difficulty cutting his food, so without fanfare I did it for him. During those days, I was impressed with Stephen's ability to cope with life and his appropriate interaction with his fellow travelers. I especially noticed his expressions of appreciation for kindness shown to him.

When my tour of duty was over, we repacked clothes for two seasons for five people, and all the keepsakes five people had decided we couldn't leave Australia without. Stephen and his father, Ed, called at our apartment where ten bulging suitcases and five strained carry-ons sat in the living room. The purpose of the call was to deliver a gift Stephen had made for me. Ed explained that his son's job was creating doormats from strips of truck tires connected with colored beads. Stephen walked through the door carrying the wrapped gift. He told me that he had made me a doormat to bring to America. He reported that he got into trouble because he took too much time to make it nice for his friend from America.

I was warmed by his kindness. Noting our over-packed luggage, his dad apologetically told me that if I needed to leave the doormat behind, that would be fine. I quickly responded, "If I have to pay Quantas Airlines extra to get it home, I will."

When we got home, I put the mat at our front

"I KNEW YOU WERE MY BEST FRIEND, BUT I DIDN'T KNOW I WAS YOURS."

door. Our guests learned about my Australian friend who made it for me and got chewed out by his supervisors because he took too long to do it right for his American friend.

A PERSON without a disability can be the catalyst of making the community more inclusive of persons with disabilities.

A few years later, a Crossroads group came to the United States. (The makeup of this group was similar to the one we accompanied to the outback.) I assisted with their travel plans while they were in our area. One day my wife and I traveled with them to show off our Great Smoky Mountain National Park, which is some forty miles from our house. As we were returning and approached the turn for our street, I remembered Stephen's gift. I asked the bus driver if he could get the bus into our subdivision. He assured me he could, and he did. When we stopped in front of our house, I asked Stephen to come with me. As we walked up our front walk, he spied his gift. He stopped, held my arm, and said, "I knew you were my best friend, but I didn't know I was yours."

TWELVE STEPS TO FRIENDSHIP

Friendship is essential to human development; we need each other. People with disabilities need friendships with people who do not have disabilities. Building a friendship with a person with a disability requires awareness of twelve basic issues.

STEP ONE   Our friends with disabilities need us to take the lead. It is true that no man is an island, but our friends with disabilities live with circumstances that separate them from others. They need bridge builders who are willing to overcome these cir-

cumstances—to come to their islands. Stephen and I
became friends when I noticed him and took the
initiative.

No matter how well-intentioned you may be, you STEP TWO
need to recognize that society's reactions to persons
with disabilities may have influenced your percep-
tions. Consider these all-too-usual events:

- The server in a restaurant asks the mother of a
  twenty-year-old man with Down syndrome what
  he wants to eat.
- In the presence of a teenager with behavior problems, a relative talks about how awful he is and
  predicts the bleakness of his future.
- Noticing the customer is blind, the clerk in the department store talks louder.
- A once-active man, who uses a wheelchair as the
  result of a spinal injury, is ignored by his friends.
- A Christian education director doesn't see the
  value of developing the spiritual lives of persons
  with disabilities in his congregation's Sunday
  school.

Analyzing these reactions suggests that people
with disabilities are not seen as real people. The im-
plications of the reactions are obvious:

- They have lost their humanity.
- They are single-dimensioned people without
  feeling.
- They are just there.
- Someone else will answer for them.
- They are all alike.
- Not hearing, not seeing, not understanding result
  in the same problems.
- Talking louder will solve the communication
  problems.

These reactions worsen the situation. The person without a disability feels awkward and helpless. The person with a disability feels isolated and ignored.

STEP
THREE

In order to build a friendship with a person with a disability we must learn to respond to facts and not to feelings. Note the following facts:

- People with mental retardation are clever and enjoy friendship.
- People who have emotional problems do have feelings.
- People who are blind have lost only one sensory modality.
- People with physical disabilities learn new activities and still can be included in the old ones.
- Everyone can develop spiritually.

STEP
FOUR

Your friendship will be easier to build if you understand why there is now more openness toward people with disabilities. In recent times American communities have experienced some positive strides toward including the disability community. The beginning of the change occurred in 1975 when the Congress passed Public Law 94-142, the Mandatory Education Act for all children with disabilities. (It was changed in 1990 and is now called IDEA: Individuals with Disabilities Education Act.)

The part of IDEA most relevant to our discussion is the "least restrictive environment" section. Simply stated, the law mandates that the child with a disability be educated in his neighborhood school with his age-mates.

As the law was enacted, terminology changed. "Mainstreaming" gave way to "inclusion" and now we deal with "full inclusion." Coupled with the 1990 Americans with Disabilities Act, the education law set the stage for more inclusion. Additionally, the Special Olympics demonstrated that our friends with disabilities enjoy sports competitions—just like the rest of us. The legal community has provided impetus for more inclusion. The concept of equality under the law continues to expand.

Realize that the concept of inclusion is a valid one. **STEP FIVE** Segregation doesn't build friendships. Inclusion is more than politically correct. It is more than an "in" word. Inclusion will make a difference now and in the future. When a student with a disability is known by his peers, relationships will develop—relationships that can have lifelong effects.

Consider the doctor who, when in the seventh grade, was a peer tutor to a fellow student with cerebral palsy. Many years later when he returns to his hometown to practice medicine, he sees his friend on the street, and greets him. He doesn't ignore him. They find that they attend the same church. Word spreads, and people with disabilities are welcomed in his practice.

Consider also the recreation director who had been a chemistry partner with a student with spina bifida. Working in her vocation, the director remembers the accommodations required by her classmate and works to provide them in her programs.

In any relationship it is good to remember that we **STEP SIX** learn from each other. When I went to school, I had friends who modeled good behaviors, taught me the rules of friendship, invited me to parties, asked me to go to church, and shared ideas—all of which helped me develop. Our friends with disabilities need good role models too. But while we are modeling skills they may have missed, courtesy demands that we treat them with respect and be ready to learn from their unique perspective on the world.

STEP SEVEN   The community will not open automatically for a person with a disability. As the person makes inroads into the community, he will need friends to assist with removing barriers, blazing trails, and creating positive encounters. Such friends must be prepared to make a consistent commitment to the process.

This issue of removing barriers is so important to inclusion that Congress now requires the school system to develop a transition plan to help students enter their communities. When the mandatory education act was revised in 1990 and 1996, legislators noted that following graduation, many students were not integrated into their communities. To correct this situation, the school system must now arrange a plan for the student to work, to have a place to live, and to receive future education in the community by the time he is fourteen.

Unfortunately, even with this transition plan and more than twenty-five years of experience with the inclusion concept, the community at large is not always friendly and responsive to persons with disabilities. The natural interaction of peers without disabilities is inconsistent or lacking altogether.

An interested, available person offering friendship will promote a natural entrance and integration into the community. The many facets of community life will open to our friends with disabilities when we clear the path and provide the opportunities.

STEP EIGHT   The facets, or scope, of disability offer a variety of opportunities for involvement. Three facets worthy of note are severity, time of onset, and immediacy.

The severity of the diagnosis dictates the level of friendship. Two of my dearest friends have cerebral palsy. One of them, now deceased, couldn't walk. Her schooling was limited to special education. Her experiences were limited. My wife and I were consistently involved in her life with visits, gifts, and cards.

Our other friend walks. She is working on a second college degree. She skydives. (See chapter six.) Our friendship is based on mutual interest in disability issues and her training for a future vocation in the field.

The time of life when a disability occurs also regulates the friendship demands. A head injury that occurs when a person is sixteen will require retraining in new surroundings and unfamiliar faces. A supportive friend from his old world would be an asset. Former friends from car-pooling days should continue to support the young wife who can no longer care for her children or manage her household because of a stroke.

Finally, reaching out to a friend with a disability is easier when you recognize the immediacy of disability. Each of us is a heartbeat away from a stroke, an automobile accident, or a fall that could leave us with a disability.

A person without a disability can be the catalyst for making the community more inclusive of persons with disabilities. The special education student needs a place to practice skills learned in the classroom. An adult with traumatic brain injury can use an arena to relearn old skills and learn new ones. A couple adjusting to the changes brought about by the birth of a child with a disability would welcome assistance in adjusting to new approaches to life. Programs are available, but a warm, pulsating human can enhance the process and make a difference.

STEP NINE

Be sensitive and aware of the people with disabilities you see around you. While ordering lunch at a fast-food restaurant, I noticed that the employee had mental retardation. When she asked me if my order was for the dining room or takeout, I said dining room. She prepared my food to take out. A supervisor

STEP TEN

noticed the mistake and asked her to change it. I said, "Please don't. I can carry the sack to the table as easily as a tray. After all, I may not have made myself clear."

STEP ELEVEN   Use your profession to form friendships. For example, I have a schoolteacher friend who takes students home with her for weekend visits to assist them in practicing the concepts they have learned in class that week. A doctor might invite a patient with cerebral palsy to lunch. For inclusion in the community to work, the person with a disability must be surrounded by understanding friends who care and want to make a difference.

STEP TWELVE   Realize that the person with a disability needs to have his spiritual being nurtured. Church growth surveys indicate that the main reason a person attends church is not the minister, not the choir, not the youth program, but a friend or relative who invited or was influential in bringing the person. Could it be that more persons with disabilities would attend church if they had a friend to invite them? The church deals with matters of eternal importance, offers a reason to hope, and purpose for living. These things are just as vital to a person with a disability as to one without. A friend is one who introduces another to the church and to Jesus Christ.

These are the twelve basic steps to friendship. They are not far different from the steps you would take with any person. Now you are ready to share friendship with real people who happen to have disabilities. They are more like us than different. They can be reached by telephone. They have addresses. They sneeze, cry, get sick, like hamburgers, giggle, forget, and do other things people without disabilities do. They have names!

CHAPTER 2

FRIENDSHIP ADVENTURES

His name is Tom. He is a resident of Riverwood Christian Community, a group home for adults with mental retardation in Louisville, Tennessee. He has helped me learn that faith is immediate. The truth that God is with us is valid today. The Bible means what it says.

I enjoy Tom Keck. We are good friends. I genuinely like him. Unless I, as director of the community, have to talk sternly to him about his behavior on his job, I think he feels the same way about me.

Much of my friendship with Tom has centered around trips—first to visit his parents, then to visit his widowed mother, and now to put flowers on his parents' graves in Johnson City, Tennessee. If Tom knows the trip plan, he is more relaxed. He finds comfort in knowing what is going to happen, so, our trips start with an explanation of our route and plan of travel. For example, I would tell Tom, "We are going to get on Interstate 40 and go to Interstate 81. We will stay on it until it becomes Interstate 181. We will take the Roan Street exit, then go on to your parents' house. Because your mother is preparing lunch for you, we won't stop to eat today. We will stop only to get a cup of coffee. Is it your turn to buy or mine?"

Interestingly, when we stop to get a beverage, Tom

announces our schedule to the clerk. Often I have heard him add to the travel report the menu of the meal we had just eaten, "I had two cheeseburgers, fries, and a large Coke. Dr. Pierson (or however he was addressing me at the time) had a chicken sandwich and a diet Coke."

En route, he waves at every eighteen-wheeler, every car with law enforcement ID, and every emergency vehicle. Occasionally, if he notices the highway sign indicating we are entering a different county, he will ask, "Who is the sheriff of this county, anyway?" He knows the names of sheriffs in several counties. His favorite lunch place is one frequented by truckers and that serves mashed potatoes with gravy and macaroni and cheese. Tom will say, "These are my kind of people."

> "My name *is* Tom. I *was born with Down syndrome. What were you born with?*"

Tom knows who he is. He is aware that he has a disability. He remarked to a man he had just met, "My name is Tom. I was born with Down syndrome. What were you born with?"

Tom was born in 1949. Knowing that date is important because it means that in 1975, when the Mandatory Education Act was passed, Tom was twenty-six years old—well past school age and too old to benefit from the new law. In his childhood, special education services were limited and often difficult to obtain. However, his mother was a schoolteacher and gave her son a wonderful skill—he can read! He reads the newspaper, news magazines, and signs on doors. For the person who doesn't know of his skill, Tom is a puzzle. He once visited my parents in their assisted-living facility and immediately addressed them by their first names. Mother was amazed. "How does he know our names?" she asked. I nodded to the nameplates on their door.

Tom has a great deal of interest in knowing how old people are—actually, he has an obsession! He approaches his goal in several ways: "How old are you now?" he will ask. "How much older are you than me? When is your next birthday?" Once at Riverwood we wanted to impress a lady who was visiting. Remembering Tom's "hobby," I cautioned him not to ask her how old she was. Tom agreed. When she arrived, Tom appeared to greet her. I gave him my sternest stare. My stare was interrupted by Tom's question, "How much do you weigh now?"

His sense of humor is unpredictable. Most of the time, when he sees a friend he gets straight to what he wants to know. Sometimes he will report what is going on at church, or work, or at the group home. At Riverwood functions, he is often called on to pray. People are moved to tears by the sincerity of his prayers. On one occasion when Tom was invited to pray, he made a wild bowing gesture and said, "As the skunk said, 'Let us spray.'" Then he started to pray! The residents took it in stride, and the staff managed not to interrupt Tom's prayer with laughter.

He never meets a stranger. He will talk to anyone, anywhere. A waitress will know about his parents' death, the funeral

"DAD AND MOM ARE NOT HERE. THEY ARE IN HEAVEN. WHEN I DIE, I WILL GO TO HEAVEN. WE WILL ALL BE TOGETHER AGAIN."

home who did the service, who officiated, and then he will announce the plans for his own funeral. Then, because they are so wide-eyed with all of the information that Tom thinks they are interested, he will give the details of the trip we are on, what time we left, where we have stopped, how many trucks we have passed.

He is fun to be around. He is pleasant, asks appropriate questions (most of the time), enjoys his friends, and is easy to entertain. When he stays overnight at our house, he finds something to read, checks what's on television, asks for a video, or just goes to his room. If the visit is during the weekend, he always has his Bible and glasses to take to church with him. He likes to read his Bible, and does it often.

> "WE ARE *dealing with a little baby we love, not a sack of potatoes.*"

Tom's history is interesting. He was adopted as a baby. When his disability was discovered, the adoption agency asked Mr. and Mrs. Keck if they wanted to send him back. The stunned parents replied, "We are dealing with a little baby we love, not a sack of potatoes."

The Kecks reared Tom in an atmosphere that communicated to him their love, their care, and their respect for his person. These gifts will sustain him throughout his life. In addition to the reading skills from his mother, his minister father gave him a deep faith in God, an understanding of who Jesus is, and a devotion to the church. Being exposed on a regular basis to congregations in several states, Tom understands what church is about. He sees himself as a preacher. When he prays his beautiful prayers, it is obvious that he understands the language of the church.

The reason I traveled with Tom so often was his parents' belief that they needed to be together. They were one hundred miles away in a retirement community. He was in a group home. As long as they were able, they came to see him. When they were no longer able to visit, I took Tom to them. After his father's death, I continued to take him to see his mother. If she was in the hospital, we would make trips at her request or on holidays. Since her death, Tom enjoys going to put flowers on the graves of both his parents.

During these latter trips, the real value of Tom's heritage from his father became abundantly clear. Tom believes that God will take care of him. The depth of his faith is illustrated by his understanding of death, and life after death. When his father died I drove Tom to the funeral. As we traveled, I asked him what the happiest memory of his father was. He answered, "The day he baptized me." The discussion that followed proved that poor cognitive skills had not kept Tom from developing outstanding Christian beliefs. At the funeral home, the staff arranged for Tom to view his father in private. After some time, I stepped into the room and asked him how he was doing. He answered, "Fine. Dad's not here. He is in Heaven. Someday my mom will die and go to Heaven. When I die, I will go to Heaven. Then, we will all be together again."

When his mother died a few years later, I gave him the news, "Your mother died in her sleep last night."

Tom responded, "She's with Jesus."

> TOM BELIEVES *that God will take care of him. The depth of his faith is illustrated by this understanding of death, and life after death.*

On the first trip to put roses on his parents' graves, Tom asked me if he could talk to them. "Sure," I answered. "Do you want me to go to the car and wait for you?"

"No, you stay," he instructed. The words that followed were not ones I had often heard from Tom. They were angry words, full of hurt and fear. I was concerned, but I knew his faith. On a later visit I heard, "Hi, Mom, Dad, I'm doin' OK. I miss you. I will come to be with you someday." I knew his faith was making the difference.

When Tom enters a new phase of his life, he is often uncertain, but he always seems to grasp what he needs to do. I was with him when he was fitted for a hearing aid. As usual, he charmed those working with him, appeared fearful, but in the end accepted the situation in good form. It is his faith in God that gives him courage. He knows, even through a limited intellect, that God loves him and cares for him.

I have traveled to twenty-five countries and many of the fifty states, but when I reflect on all my trips, I realize that some of the most spiritually and personally enriching ones have been with my good friend, Tom Keck.

BEFRIEND A PERSON WITH MENTAL RETARDATION

Find a friend like Tom. Having someone like him in your life will be a mutually fulfilling experience. A friendship with a person with mental retardation is easy to develop if you have some awareness of the symptom. Notice I use the word "symptom." Mental retardation is the result of lack of oxygen at birth, a blow to the head, an extra chromosome, a frayed chromosome, or similar condition. Some points will be helpful in leading you to befriend a person with mental retardation.

POINT ONE   Mental retardation happens to individuals. They are not all the same. Their personalities, attitudes, approaches to life are as different as those of people without disabilities.

They learn slowly and never achieve age level abilities. Most of them, about 85 percent, are able to do two of the three R's fairly consistently. They can read—perhaps not many paragraphs with understanding—but short instructions and directional signs. They may write their names, addresses, and notes to friends. The "R" they have trouble with is arithmetic. Few accomplish the most practical mathematical concepts, like understanding money. Keeping a checkbook balanced is not a part of their résumé.

POINT TWO

They don't retain as much information as their age-mates. They don't reason well. They don't think quickly on their feet. However, having mental retardation doesn't mean they are stupid. As a matter as fact they can be clever, joke, have hobbies, and enjoy friendship. One of my most pleasant memories of one of my friends with mental retardation was his delight in reading "knock-knock" jokes. His poor comprehension skills kept him from understanding most of the punch lines, but his laughter brought happiness to his friends, and their response encouraged him all the more.

POINT THREE

The big problem in developing relationships with people with mental retardation is the difference in mental age that dictates their interest levels. Note the following areas of daily living.

POINT FOUR

- Family—Because they can't handle the responsibility of marriage, most people with mental retardation do not marry.
- Residence—Most often, they live at home with their parents. Some are in group homes, sheltered apartments, or other special living options.
- Jobs—If they work, it is in a sheltered workshop or in a supported employment setting. With the

change in employment opportunities some are working in regular jobs and may even be in a co-operative where they earn some profits from the business.

- Recreation—Much of their playtime is with groups or their families. They enjoy being spectators at sporting events. They like amusement parks. They like to go to museums. They like to do the same kinds of things we do. Special Olympics is a part of many of their lives.

- Church—While the situation is improving, people with mental retardation do not have ready access to the church. They need a friend to provide entry into the church experience.

POINT
FIVE

Knowing the definition of mental retardation will enhance understanding of our friends who have the symptom. The accepted definition has three parts. First, the person has low intellectual functioning (an IQ of 69 or below). Second, he will have deficiencies in adaptive behaviors. Third, the cause of the mental retardation happens before the person's eighteenth birthday.

The term "adaptive behavior" deserves clarification for those who want to make friends of people with mental retardation. The concept of adaptive behavior is not a part of our everyday conversation. We don't need to *talk* about it because we can *do* age-appropriate activities. For example, I can drive a car, discuss an item on a charge that isn't mine, and balance my checkbook. I can do the things necessary to maintain my life without supervision. My friends with mental retardation can't. Adaptive behaviors are progressive. When they were little, they were late walking and talking. When they went to school, they stayed behind academically. It will be a life-long shortage. However, having a helpful friend can lead to more development and opportunity.

The emotional state of a person with mental retardation needs to be taken into consideration. They are not always predictable. They are not mentally ill, but don't have an easy way to express frustration—which they feel a lot. They lack a language system that allows them to be calmed. For example, if I am crying and a friend explains the facts of a situation, I am soothed by his insight. I can reason. My friends with mental retardation don't reason well. Look beyond the behaviors and see the real person. The negative traits often keep people from seeing the positive ones. It is simple; if the person always is corrected for a bad behavior and gets no recognition for a good one, the bad behavior will continue because it is his only way of getting attention. **POINT SIX**

They are not always neat and do not possess the best manners. Having a friend to monitor them will improve both. They need a little help and some reminders about introducing their friends to you, how to enter a conversation, how to end a conversation, or how to order food at a restaurant. Help them with the basics. Your assistance will help them become socially competent. **POINT SEVEN**

Armed with this information, you are ready to befriend a person with mental retardation. Don't let fear keep a friendship from developing. Such fears as, "I won't be able to talk to him," "She might act out," "I won't know what to do if something goes wrong," "He might have a seizure," will all be relieved as you get to know the person.

HOW DO YOU ESTABLISH A FRIENDSHIP WITH A PERSON WITH MENTAL RETARDATION?

Locate a person with mental retardation who needs friendship. About one percent of the people living in your community have mental retardation. **STEP ONE**

With such a number, all you have to do is look. Look in your neighborhood. Perhaps you have noticed a person at the bus stop, a fellow diner in your favorite restaurant, or the employee who cleans the floor at McDonald's. A greeting as simple as, "My name is Jim, what's yours?" could be the start of a meaning-ful friendship. Another approach is to go into the community where they are. Volunteer for Special Olympics. Visit a group home. Go to a sheltered workshop or sheltered apartment. Social workers can provide names of people who need some atten-tion. I know a doctor and a minister who regularly provide friendship to a man with mental retardation whose family is dead. Just look: there are many peo-ple who need your friendship.

STEP
TWO
Visit with the person in his residence. Get to know his family support system. Who is the most responsi-ble for his care? How often does the family visit? Is the family gone?

STEP
THREE
Learn something about his diagnosis. Down syn-drome and Fragile X are two common ones. The li-brary will give good detail. If you are on-line, just type in the diagnosis and you will receive a lot of in-formation. Always remember: mental retardation happened to a real person who has a name.

STEP
FOUR
Get to know his world. What is his day like? Where does he work? What does he do when he isn't at work? What are his hobbies? What does he collect?

STEP
FIVE
Let him know your world. Your family. Your job. Your church. Your friends.

STEP
SIX
Communicate honestly. Don't say you understand his speech when you don't. The longer you know the person, the easier his speech will be to understand.

Your friend will be happy to help you learn his way of communicating.

Find a common interest. Develop visits around this common interest. Go to a hockey game. Go to a concert. Go to a movie.

STEP SEVEN

Make the friendship as equal as possible. For example, take turns paying for food and beverages, the entrance fees to movies and other outings. Be sensitive to low wages or the lack of money in general. But allowing your friend to buy you a cup of coffee will do a lot for his self-esteem. One of my favorite activities with a friend of mine who has mental retardation is to have coffee with him. Our time together is enhanced by his delight in determining whose turn it is to pay. By the way, many entertainment places have special rates for persons with disabilities. Find out in advance and make arrangements on behalf of your friend.

STEP EIGHT

Invite your friend to church and offer him a ride. This may involve learning how to disassemble and reassemble his wheelchair or folding walker. Check beforehand to make sure that your church building is accessible.

STEP NINE

Enjoy your friend. Learn from him as he learns from you. I hope your friendship adventure will be as wonderful as mine has been with Tom. Our relationship brings me pleasure, smiles, reinforcement of eternal truths, the knowledge of people's age, and a travel companion.

STEP TEN

CHAPTER 3

PRACTICE LOOKING AT THE HEART

Her name is Dory—well, really, Dorothy Miller. When I hear the words "snicker doodle," "bumps," "mayor," or "inner beauty," I think of Dory. All of those words are key to knowing who she was. But the ones that were most important to knowing her were "inner beauty."

Dorothy Miller was one of the first residents to live at Riverwood. I learned about her through letters from her parents and a couple from her. Prior to the day she came for an interview, I knew from the information in her folder that her diagnosis was von Recklinghausen's disease. I knew her father was a minister. I knew her parents wanted her to continue to develop as a person.

When she walked into my office for the interview, it was obvious that the benign tumors of von Recklinghausen's disease had disfigured her appearance. She was slightly stooped, one side of her face seemed drawn, and the fibroma (bumps consisting mainly of fibrous tissue) covered her visible skin. Looking at her was confirmation of the diagnosis. I had no trouble believing her parents' reports of stares, unkind comments, and rejection since most people rely on the external to make judgments. Inwardly, Dory had

INWARDLY, DORY HAD
NO BUMPS—SHE CARRIED
HERSELF WITH GRACE AND
DIGNITY.

no bumps—she carried herself with grace and dignity.

Accepted to live at Riverwood, she was a leader, and the other residents knew it. She was elected Riverwood's first mayor. Her ability to read was an asset to her leadership in a group of many nonreaders. Like any good leader, she had personal goals. When I asked what she wanted to achieve by living at Riverwood, she knew! "I want a roommate. I want a boyfriend. I want a job in a print shop. I want to go to a church where my dad isn't the preacher."

Dory was really into being a resident. She worked at it. Her four goals were accomplished. She and her roommate enjoyed each other and enjoyed girl talk. One Christmas break, Dory invited her roomie to spend the holidays with her in West Virginia. She enjoyed her boyfriend too. Their relationship consisted mainly of sitting together in church, playing a game together, or just talking. There were times of showing off a piece of jewelry he had given her.

The job in a print shop seemed an unreachable goal until I got a telephone call from a printer. We were discussing a newsletter he was printing for us. Before hanging up, he added, "We want to hire one of your residents. We will be glad to train the person. Let me know if you ever have someone." I replied, "I have someone now." Dory loved her job.

First Christian Church in Maryville, Tennessee, had a minister who wasn't her father. She enjoyed the people who responded to her and her fellow residents with gracious acceptance.

The residents enjoyed her. She talked about exciting things from her reading. She enjoyed her environment and it showed. Residents considered her a good friend. The length of her friendship roster may have been due in part to her culinary skills; her snicker doodle cookies were delicious.

Dory reminded me of Dorcas in the New Testament. She had several handwork skills she put to use for her friends. Gifts from her were standard to her method of operation. To this day my desk displays a nameplate she cross-stitched for me.

The residents saw the real Dory. At a prayer meeting one of the male residents prayed, "When Dory gets to Heaven, please take away her bumps." Her fellow resident could see the results of the disease, but he also saw the person who lived with it. She was his friend, always available for a chat, a bike ride, or a walk.

THE RESIDENTS saw the real Dory. One of them prayed, "When Dory gets to Heaven, please take away her bumps."

During the interview with the admissions committee in April, 1986, an interviewer asked Dory if her home state, Michigan, was not a long way from Tennessee. "Yes, it is," she replied. "I will miss my parents and my cat, and I will be homesick, but here I will have friends." Her loneliness was deep.

At lunchtime that day I saw Dory waiting in line. I approached her to let her know that I saw her, not the tumors. A three-quarter-length sleeve made it easy to deliberately touch the tumors on her hands and arms. Looking her in the eye, I said, "Dory, you are one of the most beautiful people I have ever seen."

"Thank you, Mr. Pierson," she responded. "Most people don't get close enough to notice." I will always be grateful I did.

There is an epilogue to Dorothy's story. Because the symptoms of her disease worsened, the staff of Riverwood could not provide care for her. She was moved to a nursing home in West Virginia, where her father had moved to a new church. We knew that in her case the facts about von Recklinghausen's disease were right: death could occur by age twenty-five. A fibroma was growing toward the part of her brain that controls breathing. Her family kept us posted on her condition. When Dory's father telephoned to tell us she died, he explained that she died while sorting get-well cards with an aide at the nursing home. The fibroma had done its work. After I hung up from the conversation, a concerned staff member asked what the message was. I replied, "Dory has lost her bumps."

Dory provided a real laboratory to practice the godly quality of looking at the heart and not the outward appearance.

BECOMING ACQUAINTED WITH THE WORLD OF DISABILITY

In befriending a person with a disability, remember that disability happens to people—real, wonderful people. Knowing something about their world will also help you.

They each have a label for what they have. With Dory it was "von Recklinghausen's disease." When you find out what your new friend has, read an article about the diagnosis from a magazine in the library, check the Internet, or read an encyclopedia entry. Be careful not to look so far into the diagnosis that the person becomes a client, an object, a good example of the disorder. After you know something about the diagnosis, look inside the person, not at the external symptoms. Your friend is a person who needs to be seen for his humanity, not his diagnosis.

After speaking at a church service in Illinois, the minister and I were greeting people in the foyer. Person after person reached out to shake my hand until suddenly, there was not a hand to shake. I looked up to determine the cause for the delay and found a lady with Down syndrome eyeing me. With hands on hips, she rocked a bit and asked, "Hey, Buddy, was you the one in there talking about mental retardation and all that stuff?"

I nodded affirmatively.

"Good," she responded giving a thumbs up sign, "I am one and it is OK."

The next person in line was her mother. Wiping tears from her eyes, she said, "All of her life I have taught her that she is a valuable, wonderful person. It is good to hear you affirm it in her church."

The academic community debates the use of labels. There are pros and cons but it is really useful to know which disability you are dealing with. Just don't let knowing about it get in the way of seeing your friend as a person. Develop some knowledge of some categories of disabilities. The ones the school system uses gives us a place to start.

- **Mental retardation.** These students learn more slowly and retain less information than their age-mates. Down syndrome and Fragile X syndrome are two well-known diagnoses in this category.
- **Learning disabilities.** These children have above-normal intelligence, but have trouble learning. Academically, math and reading are difficult. Requirements to sit still and listen create social problems for them.
- **Serious emotional disturbance.** These children have such severe problems relating, behaving, coping,

and responding, that the problems interfere with education and social pursuits.

- **Visual impairment.** Children with vision difficulties fall into two groups: *visually impaired* means that the child uses large print to learn, and the child who is *blind* uses braille.
- **Hearing impairment.** Children with auditory difficulties fall into three groups: Those born without hearing and who did not develop speech are *deaf;* those who had hearing and developed speech, but lost both have been *deafened;* those whose acuity level has been weakened are *hard-of-hearing.*
- **Communication disorders.** This category includes delays in speech and language abilities. Students with speech disorders experience problems with articulation (not speaking plainly), voice (tone is not appropriate to sex and age), and fluency (stuttering). There may be receptive problems (reading and listening), in which case children with language disorders have difficulty understanding, or problems expressing themselves (speaking and writing), which create difficulties in being understood.
- **Orthopedic impairment.** Children with cerebral palsy, spina bifida, muscular dystrophy, or missing limbs are representatives of this group.
- **Other health impairment.** Children with heart problems, diabetes, asthma, and sickle cell anemia serve as examples of this category.
- **Traumatic brain injury.** Since 1990, the school system has treated TBI as a separate category. Students with head injuries caused by motor vehicle and bicycle accidents, abuse, and sports accidents are assisted with speech production, language comprehension, social skills, learning, psychological problems, and orthopedic needs.
- **Autism (pervasive developmental disorder).** When

TBI became a separate category, so did autism. Learners with a diagnosis of autism receive more focused attention on serious communication and relational deficiencies.

Another factor to take into consideration when building a relationship is the *degree* or *severity* of the disability. Problems can range from mild to severe, but no one functions at a level too low to respond to love and the warmth of caring. Include persons with all degrees of disability in your friendship outreach.

At one point in my life, I visited a lady in a nursing home on a regular basis. She did not respond to me noticeably, but I continued to go. I would talk about the day, the beauty of the season, and say a prayer. When she communicated with her family, which was rare, she spelled. After her death, her daughter reported to me that the last word she spelled was "P-I-E-R-S-O-N." Although she had never responded to me, she knew her friend was there.

> No one *functions at a level too low to respond to love and the warmth of caring.*

The age of the person with the disability determines the services available through public agencies.

- **From birth to three years of age,** early intervention developmental programs are standard. They include physical, occupational, and speech therapies, support for the family, and informational programs.
- **From three to twenty-one years of age,** the local school system is responsible for education. Governed by IDEA (Individuals with Disabilities Education Act), the child's educational needs are met if deemed appropriate by a child study committee, commonly called a multidisciplinary team.

- **After twenty-one or twenty-two,** depending when the person's birthday falls, community programs are available. These may offer work in a sheltered workshop or supported employment, and living arrangements in a group home, sheltered apartment, or supported living. The community program may assist in living at home with Mom and Dad.

RESTRICTIVE BOUNDARIES

The disability world is a world of special transportation, limited by the boundaries of the person's disability. Most people are accustomed to freedom of movement. We drive cars. Public transportation is available. A summer vacation to a warmer or colder climate is routine. People with disabilities don't move about that easily or readily. Unless family members or program staff members provide it, transportation is difficult. After the person is out of school, getting to work, to the mall, or to a sporting event generally doesn't happen without the help of a family member or friend.

Another element of the world of disability is medication. To control seizures, regulate the heart, emotions, mood swings, or a variety of ailments, your friend with disabilities takes medications. The family member, residential staff, or caregiver can tell you what the medication is and will ask that you supervise the taking of it.

Your friend's mother says he has to have medication at noon. *Oh no,* you think, *we are going to be out at lunchtime!* Not to worry, it's no big deal. Your supervision can be as easy as this actual exchange.

As my friend got into the car, I asked, "Do you have your lunch meds?" He silently patted his shirt pocket and then pulled out a small brown envelope. I said, "Good."

At lunch, before he started eating (two cheeseburgers, large fries, and a large Coke), he removed the envelope from his pocket, took the meds, said grace,
and asked me how much longer we had to drive.

The world of disability is often more medical than
the regular world. There are more situations that require a specialist. The neurologist monitors seizure
activity and the medications that control it. The orthopedist checks on curvature of the spine. A psychi-
atrist intervenes with medication and advice for
behavior problems. The cardiologist checks the heart
of your friend with Down syndrome. The nephrolo-
gist will check on a person with spina bifida's kidney
function. After a visit or two, you probably will
know the medical needs of your friend.

NOT A WEALTHY GROUP

There are not many opportunities for people with
disabilities to get money. The person may work at a
full-time job for minimum wage, which may or may
not provide some health and dental benefits. Or, the
person's money may come from a trust fund es-
tablished by his family to provide his care.

He may receive social security. There are two income support programs: Supplemental Security Income (SSI or Title IV) and Social Security Disability
Insurance Program (SSDI, Title II). There are many
factors involved with the amount of money the person receives: how much money he makes, whether he
lives at home or in special housing, whether or not
his parents are living. Often the cost of housing is re-
imbursed by the Department of Mental Health/Men-
tal Retardation (or whatever it is called in your
state).

Social security income may be supplemented by
food stamps or other applicable programs. Work
may be funded by the Department of Vocational Re-

habilitation. Health care comes through the Department of Human Resources or private insurance. Unless the parents have made provisions for their child's future, the bottom line is that there will not be much money if the person is dependent on social security.

The more you know about your friend's world the better friend you will be. You now have a general description of your friend's world. As you get to know your friend, you will add more specific information about his daily routine.

KEEPING UP WITH THE WORLD OF DISABILITY

Learning about the world of disability and keeping up with the latest developments can be a difficult job. It is an important job, however. Part of being a good friend is understanding your friend's life and world. Because materials go out of print quickly and the books don't always make it to the public library, I want to offer some practical, easy, and useful resources to stay abreast.

Church workers often report, "There just aren't any materials out there!" The truth is there are plenty of materials; the problem is knowing where to find them. The most comprehensive bibliography I know of is *Dimensions of Faith and Congregational Ministries with Persons with Developmental Disabilities and Their Families.* The latest issue (published in 1996) is from the University Affiliated Program of New Jersey in partnership with the Religious Division of the American Association on Mental Retardation. This bibliography contains books, lesson materials, children's books, videos, and publications relating to the religious nurture of persons with disabilities. A sample of the seventeen divisions of this excellent publication will suggest its value: "Architectural and Attitudinal Accessibility"; "Mission and Outreach-Inclusive Ministries"; "Religious Education Guides and Curricula"; "Resources and Guides for Families, Parents, and Friends of Persons with Developmental Disabilities"; "National Faith Group Resource and Consulting Offices." Order this reference guide from Building Community Supports Project, Post Office Box 6810, Piscataway, NJ 08855-6810.

Having a current college textbook on special education is another way of keeping up. This resource will provide you with information about various categories of students with exceptionalities, the methods and approaches used by the school system to educate them, suggestions for working with families, and the legal guidelines that govern the provision of special education. There are many good textbooks, but the one I keep nearby is the one I have used for years in teaching college students. Now in its eighth edition, *Educating Exceptional Children* is written by Samuel Kirk, James J. Gallaher, and Nicholas J. Anastasiow. Published by Houghton Mifflin, the book gives information about the eighteen years the school is mandated to educate students with disabilities. Because of the length of time involved and the value of these years to the person's development, it is essential to understand where your friend has spent or will spend much of his life.

> THE INTERNET *provides current information about specific disabilities and organizations.*

My favorite resource for staying current with the field is *Children with Disabilities*. Edited by Dr. Mark L. Batshaw, the book has grown from 664 pages to 926 pages, from the third (1992) to the fourth (1997) edition. The book is a comprehensive guide to the major disabilities and issues pertaining to them. Order it from Paul H. Brookes Publishing Company, Post Office Box 10624, Baltimore, Maryland 21285-0624. Brookes has an excellent selection of books on disability issues.

The Internet provides a lot of good information. Current information about specific disabilities and organizations serving them are at your fingertips. I find the most difficult chore is sorting through the reams of material to get what is the most helpful. Many organizations serving persons with disabilities have web pages. Check to see what free information they offer.

Other sources of help are materials written by a person with a disability. One of my favorite authors is Joni Eareckson Tada, who has written twenty-one books. Injured in a diving accident, Joni has provided the world of disability ministry with useful, insightful materials. Her books range from practical how-to guides to books about ethical issues, such as euthanasia. Request a list of her books and other materials from JAF, Post Office Box 3333, Agoura Hills, CA 91301.

> Joni Eareckson Tada has provided the world of disability ministry with useful, insightful materials.

Inspirational books often appear on the market. A classic is Dale Evans Rogers' story of her daughter Robin who was born with Down syndrome, *Angel Unaware*. I treasure my autographed copy. But the book that moves me every time I read it is *The Power of the Powerless*. First published in 1988 by *Guideposts*, it is now published by Zondervan. The book underscores the real value of people. Author Christopher de Vinck describes the influence that his brother Oliver had on his family and the public reaction to the essay about him published in *The Wall Street Journal*.

Oliver was blind, could not talk, walk, or learn. The family changed his diapers, fed him, and cared for his every need. Upon reading the account of

Oliver's life, one of Mr. de Vinck's English students called him a vegetable. Mr. de Vinck responded, "Well, I guess you could call him a vegetable. I called him Oliver, my brother. You would have loved him."

Mr. de Vinck affirmed his brother's value with these words, "Oliver was never able to *do* anything in that sense of the word. He was virtually paralyzed, but still he did so much for each one of us. He evoked the best love that was in us. He helped us to grow in the virtues of devotion, wisdom, perseverance, kindness, patience and fidelity. Without doing anything, Oliver made all of us better human beings. He taught us that the importance of service is not exclusively in doing for others but in allowing them to do for us. The meek and humble of heart do all of us a service when they call us to respond in love."

Although the account is old, my all-time favorite resource is the life of Jesus. The lessons He teaches and demonstrates are always fresh. May I suggest that you read Matthew, Mark, Luke, and John with pencil and paper in hand. Note the number of times Jesus dealt with persons with disabilities. Make lists of His approaches, His language, His methods. Jesus' example provides renewed energy, direction, and motive. His inclusive methods aim us at the most important part of our friends—their souls.

CHAPTER 4

INCLUSION: MORE THAN A METHOD

His name is Steve. I first met him when I was a graduate student at the University of Tennessee doing clinical practice in speech pathology. Each quarter my supervisor would assign a new caseload of clients. The purpose was to give me as many different children with as many different speech problems as possible to help me learn my craft.

One day early in the quarter, I walked into the waiting room and called for Stephen Burnett. My new client was a cute four year old with a ready smile and a happy face. I noticed that he looked at my mouth when I talked to him. His mother, who accompanied him, was a pleasant, attractive lady. I walked with Steve and his mother to the therapy room. Steve and I entered the room; she entered the observation area.

Our first meeting was fun; Steve and I bonded! His records said he probably had mental retardation. After two weeks, I doubted the diagnosis. I told my supervisor I thought he couldn't hear. "Well, his hearing has been checked," my supervisor informed me. "Have you had courses in audiology?" When I told him I had, he went with me to test Steve's hearing. My guess was right; he had a severe hearing loss.

So, Steve's therapy goals changed. I taught him speech, reading, and language skills, and worked to provide him with information he needed, such as the difference between up and down, left and right, large and small. I remember the day he learned the concept of shadow.

THIS determination to overcome barriers and get the help her son needed was exactly the kind of strength I would see in Steve.

We were working outside that day so Steve could practice identifying colors. We had worked inside using cards to learn the basic colors. Then we went out in the warm, fall sunshine to carry over the lesson. Steve was to pick out the blue cars, green cars, and the red cars.

As he strolled behind me, I thought his interest was waning because he was looking down and would occasionally make a little jump. After watching carefully for a moment, I realized he was trying to step on my shadow. He wasn't playing, nor being noncompliant. He was learning a new concept. Color was no longer as interesting to him as the gray thing that moved every time his therapist did. Holding his face in my hands, I said, "Steve, that is a shadow." With a puzzled look, he attempted to say the word. I changed my lesson plan. Steve needed to know what a shadow was. In view of the renowned Neyland Stadium where the Tennessee Volunteers would be playing football the next day, my little friend learned what a shadow was.

First, I had him repeat the word "shadow" until he could produce it on command. Then I showed him several examples of shadow: mine, his, a car's, a tree's, a building's. He was delighted. Then I had him show me shadows. He started with his own, and giggled with glee when it moved every time he did. Then he pointed out mine, a student's (who was late for class), a building's and again, his! When we returned to the waiting area of the speech and hearing center, his mother was waiting to drive him home. As we walked to the car, Steve noticed his mother's shadow. Getting her attention, he pointed to her shadow and explained, "That is you shadow." The concept had been learned. There were some later refinements of the concept, but he had the basics.

INESTIMABLE INVOLVEMENT

Steve had a wonderful family. Freda, his mother, drove him from a nearby town for therapy. She mentioned one day what time she left home. When I asked why she left so early, she told me that she was still learning to drive and had not yet mastered parallel parking. So she parked several blocks away because it was easier to park in a less-congested area. This determination to overcome barriers and get the help her son needed was exactly the kind of strength I would see in Steve.

His father, Raymond, was also heavily involved with his son's life. Three sisters also helped him. Today, two of them are in special education professions. As I worked with Steve, my relationship with these wonderful people developed to the point that his maternal grandmother tatted lace for my daughters' dresses.

When it came time for Steve to go to public school, the recommendation was for him to go to a school for the deaf. I disagreed. I reasoned that because of his high intellect, his supportive family, and his desire to learn, his neighborhood school was the best option. Because inclusion was not in vogue in those days, a critic asked, "Who will provide the support service he needs?"

"I will," I answered. And for the first four years of his elementary days, I went to his school to talk with teachers and his fellow students about my friend and his needs. My professional role changed from therapist, to consultant, to advocate, but whatever the role, I enjoyed Steve. One problem we had to solve in those early days was keeping him from making his hearing aid squeal, especially in church. He knew just where to place his hand to get the desired result!

Only one real problem surfaced during his high school years. He wanted to play in the band, but his doctor said he should not. I helped him understand that the doctor was correct. The loud sounds of the band probably would not be good for what hearing he had left. After a tear or two he agreed, but this incident wasn't to be his last try at music.

Another potential problem arose early in high school—Steve fell in love. I explained to him that I didn't deal with matters of the heart, but Steve evidently didn't need anyone's help; he is happily married to Lisa. Their daughter, Abigail, adds a special sparkle to the Burnett household.

When I went to his high school graduation, Susan, one of his sisters, commented that I shouldn't be sit-

"WHEN I WENT TO MEMPHIS I WAS PRAYING FOR A MIRACLE. I JUST DIDN'T KNOW THE MIRACLE HAD ALREADY HAPPENED."

ting with his mother. When I asked her why, she assured me that I would soon learn the reason. Sure enough, when the principal called his name to get his diploma, Steve hesitated. The therapist in me wanted to rush to explain, "He didn't understand his name." Was I ever wrong! The hesitation was to allow time for the principal to place the stole of the National Honor Society on his shoulders. Susan was right; his mother and I cried together. It was a proud moment.

Steve wanted to go to college. An evaluation by a funding agency did not recommend any funds because, they said, he could never graduate. His chosen field of study *was* a bit unusual considering his disability: he wanted to study music! When I asked him why, he responded, "God wants me to." At the end of his senior year, my wife and I went to hear him sing his senior voice recital, which he did in two languages.

Later, after his graduation I went to his hometown, to hear a Christmas cantata he directed. I was impressed, proud, and pleased that this talented young man had not allowed a hearing problem to stop him from meeting a goal. The music was stirring. As I complimented him and the choir, Steve responded, "I only wish I could hear it."

RECOGNIZING GOD'S HAND

Shortly after his graduation, Steve's parents took him to Memphis for an evaluation by a world-renowned hearing specialist. During the time I had worked with Steve, they had asked several times about the possibility of reversing Steve's hearing loss, but I didn't know of any information that would help and didn't want them or him to be disappointed. But, they decided they would feel better if they went. Many people in their church and other churches were praying for God to work a miracle.

When the doctor finished the evaluation, he couldn't believe Steve had finished a degree in music, much less that he was pursuing a career in church music. He noted that most patients with Steve's level of hearing loss would have been educated in a school for the deaf. When he asked the family their reason for Steve's not attending the school for the deaf, they told him about my suggestion that he go to regular school with his peers. The doctor told Steve to go home and thank that therapist for his suggestion.

Steve followed the doctor's orders. He came by to thank me. Then he added a statement I will never forget: "Mr. Pierson, when I went to Memphis I was praying for a miracle. A lot of people were praying with me for a miracle. I just didn't know the miracle had already happened."

I have a copy of the ontologist report from March 26, 1984. It reads in part, "You have a very severe high tone nerve type hearing loss in both ears with poor comprehension, present at birth for no apparent reason, for which there is no medical or surgical treatment possible." The doctor advised, "You should sit in the front row of church and other such public meetings, near enough to get a good look at the lips and face of the speaker. Avoid large groups and public meetings where you are at a disadvantage trying to understand what is being said." But Steve had other ideas. He didn't avoid crowds, he went to college and earned his Master's Degree in music. He doesn't sit on the front row at church, he sits on the stage as minister of music. Against all odds, he succeeded.

Once his father asked, "Jim, why did this happen to our Stephen?" I reminded him of Jesus' answer to that question. When asked why the man was born blind, Jesus said it wasn't anything the man or his parents had done.

"Then, why?" his disciples demanded.

Jesus responded, "This happened so that the work of God might be displayed in his life" (John 9:3).

As I reflect on my career, I can see that the life of Stephen Burnett has made me a better person. Steve, it is a pleasure to stand in your shadow.

JESUS' INCLUSION METHODS ARE VALID TODAY

Steve is included in his world. He is independent and participates fully in his community and profession. His family and friends have helped with this process. Inclusion is the process of offering more independence and more complete participation in the community.

Being a part of the community makes people feel better about themselves, gives them more purpose to their lives, and provides them with more opportunities to develop their God-given potential. However, the laws that have made the community more accessible to persons with disabilities do not address their spiritual needs. The church has a higher law and a stronger example to govern her actions.

Jesus evoked the inclusion process in His mission statement to His followers before He returned to his Father: "Go ye into all the world, and preach the gospel to *every* creature" (Mark 16:15, *King James Version,* my emphasis). There is no footnote about exclusions, no suggestion that too much or too little ability makes a difference, no disclaimer. Everyone needs the gospel.

As followers of Jesus, we need to study His approaches, methods, and attitudes. His inclusion skills will add to ours.

People with disabilities were a major part of Jesus' ministry. Recognizing His concern for them, people with disabilities came to Him in droves: "[Jesus] went up on a mountainside and sat down. Great crowds came to him, bringing the lame, the blind, the crippled, the mute and many others, and laid them at his feet; and he healed them" (Matthew 15:29, 30). The fact that He was *seated* suggests to me that He dealt with each case individually, not the whole lot at the same time.

I imagine a young husband and wife approaching the seated Includer. She carries a six-month-old girl who was born without vision. The child's father asks, "Will You make our daughter see?"

> INCLUSION *is the process of offering more independence and more complete participation in the community.*

Jesus reaches for the baby and asks, "What is her name?"

"Rebekah," says her mother as she gently places the baby in His arms.

"Do you have other children?"

"No," sighs the mother.

Jesus turns to the father, "What is your trade?"

"I am a carpenter."

Jesus smiles. "I learned that trade." He pulls the blanket away from the baby's face, touches His finger to His tongue, and touches her eyes, asking God to open her eyes. The father and mother hold each other tightly. Jesus smiles.

NOTABLE PRINCIPLES

Jesus' methods reflect notable inclusion principles. First, He involved the person with the disability in the ministry process. He didn't discuss the case with a committee, or even launch a plan of His own. He asked what the person wanted. Jesus asked a man with a physical disability if he wanted to be healed (John 5:6) and a man who was blind what he wanted Him to do for him (Mark 10:51). He involved the person in the ministry plan! Jesus' approach suggests the focus of ministry should be *with* the person, not *to*. The Christian should ask his friend with a disability what he needs. Be direct with your friend. Ask what you can do to help.

A second principle our Lord models is a quick, personal, and thorough response to need. Luke noted that Jesus stopped in mid-step when He heard a man who was blind call for help (Luke 18:40). When the man with leprosy felt Jesus' touch, he knew real inclusion (Luke 5:12-14). When Jesus healed the blind man and the healing was incomplete, Jesus went to all sorts of trouble to stay with him until he could see. He repeated the process. He led him outside the village. He was involved! Jesus' example is a good one for us.

Jesus believed that helping people was more important than arbitrary rules and regulations. Telling a man who was paralyzed, "Pick up your mat and walk," brought down the wrath of the Pharisees. It was not right, they said, to carry a mat on the Sabbath! Jesus also followed through in His ministry. After He healed a man with a physical disability at the pool of Bethesda, Jesus later found him in the temple and discussed deeper spiritual matters with him (John 5:1-14).

Another of Jesus' inclusive ministry principles was sensitivity to the family of the person with a disability. Jesus healed a boy with epilepsy after His disciples couldn't (Mark 9:20-24). Following a stern discussion with His disciples about their inability to minister to the boy, Jesus radiated a warm concern for his parents. He asked, "How long has your son been like this?"

The father replied, "All of his life. Sometimes during his seizure he gets so close to the fire we fear he will get burned, and so close to the water we are afraid he will drown." Jesus' question is exemplary. Expressing interest in the person and his family is better than a stare or a turned head.

Sometimes parents are blamed for the disability of a child. Such an approach did not originate with Jesus. After meeting a man who was born blind, Jesus' disciples revealed that they had judgmental thoughts (John 9:1-3). Their exchange and Jesus' response provide an eternal answer to the reason for a disability. The man's condition was not due to either his sin or that of his parents. His blindness happened, Jesus said, "So that the work of God might be displayed in his life" (John 9:3). There is no reason to blame, but every reason to support the family, and to help display God's mercy, kindness, love, and hope in their lives and the life of the child.

Jesus was an includer. When responding to people with disabilities, His unconditional love was obvious. Allowing His kind of love to work in our hearts will insure the inclusion of persons with disabilities.

> JESUS WAS *an includer. When responding to people with disabilities, His unconditional love was obvious.*

Mark tells the story of the four friends who brought their colleague to Jesus (Mark 2:1-5). The popular story details how the listening crowd blocked their route to Jesus. So the four carried him to the roof, made a hole, and lowered the man to the healing presence of Jesus. Jesus responded to the faith of the friends of the man with a physical disability and brought about healing. Here is a great lesson for us: Jesus will respond to our friendship with our friend with a disability and make a difference in his life—and in ours. Christians should be eager to ignite faith on behalf of persons with disabilities so they can develop spiritually and so we, too, can grow because of their influence on us.

Doing what Jesus did will enhance friendship in the disability community. His methods have validity today with our friends with disabilities.

CHAPTER 5

RELATING WITH RESPECT

Her name is Alice. *Reader's Digest* (April, 1983) published an article about her titled, "Born Without a Face." When people heard those words, they projected puzzlement or disbelief. "You've got to be kidding," many said. But the title was an accurate description; Alice Leigh Perkins did not have a face. However, like most people I have met—with or without disabilities—Alice had something to teach me. In her case, I learned a bunch about myself. Alice was a good teacher.

Born September 6, 1975, to an eighteen year old who already had one child, and a young father who was not ready for the responsibility, Alice's rare diagnosis, midfacial cleft syndrome, made her noteworthy. The best I can do to describe her is to say that where eyes, nose, and lips should have been there was wet mucous. The best medical guess was that during the embryonic period Alice's face just stopped growing. Later, the doctors found some eye sockets and other parts under the mucous, and these aided in the construction of her face. The doctors who did the work reported she was the most severe case they had ever seen.

Even professional people had trouble looking at Alice. Nurses who cared for her would cry, leave the room, and refuse to work with her. Maintaining a professional attitude was difficult in the presence of such deformity. In the *Reader's Digest* article, Stanley Englebardt described a meeting at the hospital in which the ICU supervisor addressed this problem. "I don't want to hear any more talk about this baby's appearance," she said. "Her name is Alice, she has a purpose in this world, and we're going to treat her like any other newborn patient."

I like the advice, "Her name is Alice." But a few months later, I, like so many others, had trouble relating to Alice. While I had heard about Alice and had read stories about her in the newspapers, I had never seen her. Following some initial surgery to create a mouth and a nose, a pediatrician referred her to the children's rehabilitation center I was directing. He requested speech therapy, physical therapy, and any help we could offer the family. On the first day she came, I walked into the room to do what I had done many times before. Usually, after presiding over the introductions and formalities, I enjoyed visiting with the families, talking to the child to assure him that if the therapist didn't behave, he just needed to see me, or giving coupons for free ice cream at a nearby restaurant. On this day, when I saw Alice, I gave instructions to a speech therapist and a physical therapist and I left the room. I could not relate to that precious little girl.

When I went home that afternoon, I didn't feel fatherly, human, or Christian. My heart, a vessel of Jesus' love, should have responded.

When I went home that afternoon, I didn't feel fatherly, human, or Christian. Having three daughters who dealt with telephones, boys, and makeup should have given me some empathy. Alice had elbows and ears and beautiful blond hair which gave her human qualities. My heart, a vessel of Jesus' love, should have responded. I spent some time thinking about how to change my reaction. After all, Alice didn't decide to be born without a face, and yet I was blaming her.

THERAPEUTIC TOUCH

Returning to the office the next morning, my plan was ready. I telephoned her foster mother, now her adoptive mom, to ask her to bring Alice fifteen minutes early the next time she brought her for therapy. I am grateful she did not ask me why.

On the day of her next appointment, I went into the waiting room to get Alice for *my* therapy before she went for *hers*. I carried her into my office. None of my feelings had changed. It was not easy. I talked to her about the pictures of my girls and other mementos in my office. There was no change in my heart. As I sat down in my swivel chair behind my desk, I prayed a brief prayer, "Father, let me let her know I care."

My eyes fell on her blond hair shining in the morning sun coming through my office window. I patted the back of her head. Then it happened. I pulled my hand forward and patted the band of skin that surrounded her malformed face. Instantly, I was Daddy, a human, and a Christian. I touched her!

Touching people where

ALICE PERKINS DID NOT HAVE A FACE. HOWEVER, LIKE MOST PEOPLE I HAVE MET, ALICE HAD SOMETHING TO TEACH ME.

they are, not where we want them to be, is a therapeutic step in the right direction. It leads to friendship and relationship.

Alice is a 1997 graduate of the Tennessee School
for the Blind. What is her future? There is a new
wrinkle: she is losing her hearing. When I heard the
news, I was saddened. However, I am glad to know
that Alice's needs have been met by many people.
Her adoptive parents, Thelma and Raymond
Perkins, have led the effort. His carpenter's union
has sent many gifts of money for her care. Whatever
her future, it will be good as long as people touch
her where she is.

On her twenty-first birthday, my wife selected a
beautiful pink card to send her. I noticed it had an
embossed picture on the front. My wife explained,
"She can feel it." Putting ourselves in the other person's place will add to our skills as friends to a person with a disability.

SOME MATTERS OF ETIQUETTE

Alice's problems were so dramatic that social
workers had to talk with people before they met her
so that their initial reactions could be softened. As
was true in Alice's situation, some preparation of
"what to do" can help. Knowing a few rules of etiquette will remove awkwardness for our encounter
with a friend with a disability. With the Golden Rule
in mind, think about the following suggestions and
add some of your own.

HOW TO TALK ABOUT A DISABILITY

• Use the word "disability" rather than "handicap" to refer to your friend's disability. "Handicap"
is the correct word to use when talking about being
hampered by architectural barriers or attitudes. For

example, "Those steps are a handicap to any person using a wheelchair," or, "He is handicapped by the low expectations of his parents."

The word "handicap" has its origins in the six-teenth century when persons with disabilities were forced to beg for their livelihood. They stood on the street corners with their caps in their hands.

• Avoid the words "cripple," "crippled," "deaf and dumb," "slow," "crazy," "invalid," "acts funny," and other insensitive, archaic descriptions of disability. In the same vein, expressions like "af-flicted with," "a victim of," and "suffers from" lead to pity and sympathy, not respect and acceptance.

• Use people-first language. Don't say, "the dis-abled," "the retarded," "the cerebral palsied," "a paraplegic." Rather say, "Jim has cerebral palsy." "The child has autism." "Persons with disabilities." "Ann has a vision problem."

• Don't describe your friend with a disability as special, overly courageous, exceptionally brave, or superhuman.

• The language of assistive devices, mobility, and adaptive equipment should be kind and gentle. Choose "Fred uses a wheelchair" rather than "Fred is confined to a wheelchair"; "Joyce uses sign lan-guage" instead of "Joyce talks with her hands"; "John communicates with an electronic machine" (or the specific name of the assistive device) instead of "John uses a machine to talk."

• When conveying that the person does not have a disability, stay away from the word "normal." The terms "typical" or "a person without a disability" are more accurate and kinder. Don't overdo such concepts as "Well, we all have a disability of some kind." The person who is dealing with the loss of one of his five senses, or a physical problem that im-pedes his mobility and/or requires assistive devices will not find that comforting.

HOW TO TALK TO A PERSON WITH A DISABILITY

- Don't assume that a person with a disability other than a hearing loss can't hear. Often we respond to a person with a disability by talking louder.
- Don't assume that people with speech, hearing, or physical problems have cognitive problems as well. In other words, don't treat them as if they were less intelligent than you are.
- Don't apologize for not understanding their speech. Just ask the person to repeat what he said.
- Don't say you understand their speech when you don't. Develop a friendly response: "My ears aren't working right today—will you say that again?" "Run that by me again, please."
- If the speech is difficult to comprehend, learn to listen for the subject of the conversation. Words like "Mom," "Dad," "church," "school" will focus your understanding; then listen for action words like "went," "walked," "saw."
- If push comes to shove, use pencil and paper, or gesture wildly. Work to get the message.
- Talk directly to the person and not through a companion or a family member.
- As you learn your friend's world, the communication problems will diminish. After awhile, the comprehension level will increase and the friendship will grow.

HOW TO HANDLE A WHEELCHAIR

- The wheelchair is an extension of the person. We should call no more attention to the chair than we would to eyeglasses or a hearing aid.
- Don't lean on, hang onto, or prop your feet on the chair.
- Ask the user's permission before pushing the chair.

• Before you push, be sure the person is secure and the brake is off.

• When entering an elevator, back the chair in so that the person is not left facing the rear wall.

• If your conversation is going to last for more than a few minutes, position yourself on eye level. Don't lean over in a patronizing manner, but sit down. This is not only polite, it's a great way to prevent a sore neck!

COMMUNICATING WITH A PERSON WHO IS DEAF

• Don't talk louder.

• Face the person to give him a good view of your face. He will be reading your lips.

• Learn finger spelling and some basic signs.

• A hearing aid amplifies every sound, not just speech. Make the environment as quiet as possible.

• To get the person's attention, wave or tap him on the shoulder.

ASSISTING A PERSON WHO IS BLIND

• In conversation, do not avoid words like "see" and "look." It is OK to ask your friend, "Did you watch that special on TV last night?"

• Ask the person if you may help. If he says no, don't be unhappy. If he says yes, offer your elbow.

• If you come to a narrow passage, move your elbow back. This movement will indicate to your friend who is blind that he should step behind you. Stopping before a step or a curb will let your friend know a step or a curb is ahead, or you may say, "step," or "curb."

• If you friend has a guide dog, don't pet it. Wait until the dog is not working, and ask permission to do so.

• When greeting a person who is blind, identify

yourself and anyone with you. For example, "This is Jim Pierson. George Brown is on my left."

• When you move, inform the person who is blind either by continuing to talk as you move or by saying, "I'm over by the counter now."

• Warn your friend of any upcoming danger, such as a low ceiling, a break in the sidewalk, or an obstacle in the path of travel.

SHAKING HANDS

• The general rule is to share the same social courtesies with the person with a disability as with those without disabilities.

• If the person uses a hook, has a missing right hand, or whatever makes shaking hands awkward, extend your hand anyway. The person will use his left hand, touch your shoulder, or do whatever he does when greeting others.

• Ask the person what he wants you to do. For example, I have a friend whose paralysis starts at his shoulders. After we shook hands the first time, he asked me to put my hand on his shoulder. He has feeling there so my greeting means more.

WHEN THE PERSON WEARS A HELMET

The purpose of a protective helmet is to prevent further injury if the person falls.

• Ask your friend who wears one if he would like to remove it while seated.

• Be sure he puts the helmet on before standing.

WHEN YOUR FRIEND USES AN ELECTRONIC DEVICE

The world of technology has made many devices available to our friends. If your friend uses a language board or other electronic device:

- Learn as much about it as you can, especially how to install batteries.
- The device is an extension of the person and should not have undue attention called to it.

HOW TO ASSIST DURING A SEIZURE

- If your friend has seizures, ask him how he knows one is about to happen.
- If one occurs while you are together, be calm. Do not try to hold him, but assist him in falling safely. Don't put anything in his mouth. If he seems to have trouble breathing, turn him on his side.
- When the seizure is over, reassure the person and remind him of what was happening when the episode occurred.

A HAPPY WORD

Your goal is for your actions to be natural and spontaneous. Give yourself some time. Remember, your friend is having to learn to deal with you, too!

CHAPTER 6

LOVE, LAUGHTER, LIFE—AND HEAVEN TOO!

Her name is Helen. She was one of the most joyous people I have ever known. When Dr. Richard Beam presided at her funeral service, he remarked, "We loved Helen at our church. She brought a special joy to us all and we will miss her. Last Sunday, my sermon was about Christians who have maintained joy in adversity, and I used as illustrations saints from ancient church history. After the service one of our members said, 'It was a good sermon, but you left someone off the list of saints who maintained joy in adversity.' I said, 'Who?' He answered 'Helen Cinnamon.' Indeed, she is on the eternal ledger of those who maintained joy under adversity to the end."

I will always consider her one of the best friends I have ever had. She was an older client in the rehabilitation facility I directed. Because of severe cerebral palsy, Helen could not walk, her speech was difficult to understand, and her hand usage was poor. She received therapy to improve these skills. When placement in our program was no longer beneficial, she was referred to a sheltered workshop where she created ceramic pieces to sell. She enjoyed her work and her fellow workers.

"HELEN CINNAMON IS ON THE ETERNAL LEDGER OF THOSE WHO MAINTAINED JOY UNDER ADVERSITY TO THE END."

To express appreciation for my role in finding her a new job, she gave me a fruit basket for a 1967 Christmas present. Her act of kindness started a family tradition that lasted until her death. During Christmas week each year, my wife, daughters, grandchildren, and I went to her house for a party. Throughout the years, the giving and receiving of twenty-six fruit baskets built a lot of memories.

Another enhancing ingredient for our friendship was our attendance at the same church. In the early 1970s, Johnson Bible College started offering the course, "Teaching the Exceptional Person in the Church." To provide hands-on experience for the students, we developed a Sunday school/church program on the campus. Several people with disabilities were transported to the campus each Sunday during the school year for Bible lessons and worship. Helen was a participant.

Sally Ashby, the teacher assigned to Helen, was a wonder. Knowing that Helen couldn't read, Sally drew pictures to illustrate the major parts of our Lord's life and ministry. The gospel lessons found a place in Helen's heart, which had not been affected by the cerebral palsy. After a few lessons, Helen told her teacher she wanted to become a Christian. Wanting to be sure Helen understood the concept, Sally requested that I talk with her. I asked her why she wanted to be baptized. In labored speech, Helen responded, "Be like Jesus."

After her baptism, Helen developed her spiritual being in the Woodlawn Christian Church in Knoxville, Tennessee. The program from Johnson had been moved there to ensure year-round participation. Helen was a vibrant part of the congregation. She was an excited, generous contributor to the church's building fund. She enjoyed giving gifts to members of the church, especially for weddings and new babies, and helping people in need. Helen was an inspirational Christian. Without saying a word, she challenged her friends to her standards of life and commitment. She enriched the lives of people around her. She was a fun person. She liked to be teased. She was—from August to November—older than I am. During those months, I enjoyed calling her "the old lady." She would beam.

> *H*ER LIFE *was not one of disability, but one of ability. Helen was not a victim of cerebral palsy; she was a victorious human being.*

Her life was not one of disability, but one of ability. Helen was not a victim of cerebral palsy; she was a victorious human being. Her life was evidence that her soul had been rehabilitated by the salvation made possible by Jesus, God's Son.

Shortly before Christmas, 1994, Helen was hospitalized with pneumonia. A few days after she came home, her condition worsened. Home health care was ordered. But sometime on the morning of January 6, 1995, after her mother turned her at 6:00, and before the nurse arrived at 7:00, Helen died. When I received the message from the nurse, I wept with grief at the loss of my dear friend. My wife and I drove to her house to be with her mother. As we were seated at the kitchen table while the morticians were removing Helen's body, my grief turned into incredible joy. I remarked to her mother, "Well, we don't have to worry about Helen's residential placement. She is now living with her wonderful Lord." The physical therapy, expensive communicative devices, and other programs had not caused major changes in her functional level, but Helen's acceptance of God's gift of eternal life through his Son provided her with the ultimate in rehabilitation.

This eternal achievement for Helen began when Sally Ashby, a student teacher in Bible college, wanted her student to know about Jesus. A few days after Helen's burial, her mother gave me the set of pictures Sally had drawn to explain God's plan of rehabilitating the soul. As I looked through the pictures and the lesson plans, I rejoiced that the goals had been met. Helen's wheelchair and communication devices were no longer needed. Her soul, freed from her flawed body, had returned to its creator. As her mother continued to go through Helen's belongings, she found a letter from Sally. This Christian rehabilitator wanted to express her love for and encouragement to her client! In part the letter read, "I'm in Massachusetts this summer. I'm serving in an internship program. I'm telling people about Jesus. Helen, have you told anyone about Jesus? Are you reviewing your pictures? I've missed you, Helen, and I'm eager to see you."

Helen was a joyous person. Her life made a difference. While I will treasure the memories of the many times we spent together (especially all of those Christmases and fruit baskets), my greatest treasure is knowing that through a caring, dedicated Sunday school teacher Helen found faith, a relationship with her Lord, and now enjoys everlasting life.

Those rewards are available to everyone. There is no greater accomplishment on earth than to introduce someone to Jesus Christ. People with disabilities need a friend to make this introduction.

MAKING THE BIBLE SCHOOL
AVAILABLE TO YOUR FRIEND

The key to Helen's relationship with the Lord and to the church was the fact that she was taught—taught by a caring teacher who wanted her to know about Jesus. Work to get your friend with a disability into the Sunday school program of your church. Inclusion will be easier when the person is younger. Making him a part of the age-appropriate class now will make acceptance more natural later. In public schools he probably will be included in a regular classroom at least for part of the day. In Sunday schools, many parents will want their child included in a regular class as well.

When children of any age with disabilities are to be included in your classroom, suggest a meeting with the parents of the child, the teacher, the minister or his representative, and parents of children without disabilities. This concept is demonstrated in "Design for Teaching Learners With Disabilities," a training video available from Standard Publishing. A seven-step method enhances the process of including students with disabilities in the regular classroom.

Offer the person in charge of your congregation's education programs the following age-related suggestions to carry out these concepts.

INCLUDING THE PRESCHOOLER

If your friend is a preschooler, provide the following ideas adapted from *Tips for Teachers*.[1]

1. Obtain information about the specific diagnosis and ask parents for essential information about care.

2. Prepare the children for the experience. Brief, simple explanations are adequate: "Our friend, Joey, has cerebral palsy. The words mean that his brain was hurt and he can't walk and run as you can.

What he says isn't always clear. He is a nice boy and wants to learn about Jesus just as much as you do."

3. Be aware that most children with disabilities will need more room to move around. Accessible rest rooms, wide doors, ramps, and grab bars offer security. Make the classroom safe. Cover sharp edges.

4. Special seating for the child will not be a problem. If the youngster needs it all of the time, his family will bring it with him. If the necessary special equipment is not available, ask an adult class or group to purchase it.

5. Record emergency information. Does he have allergies? Does he choke easily? How does he communicate his needs, especially for using the toilet? Does he have significant fears? Does he wander? Is he on medication? Is he susceptible to seizures?

6. Use a variety of teaching methods to stimulate the five senses—seeing, hearing, touching, smelling, and tasting. Children of all abilities will profit from this approach.

7. Young children notice differences in others but once their curiosity is satisfied they usually will accept the difference with nonchalance, especially if the teacher is modeling an attitude of complete acceptance. Watch them react to their classmates with disabilities—they can teach adults important lessons about acceptance.

INCLUDING THE ELEMENTARY AGE CHILD

If your friend is of elementary age, present the following suggestions for including a variety of children in the Sunday school.

Students With Developmental Disabilities (Mental Retardation)

1. Routine is important. It provides stability and continuity.

2. Use concrete language. Teach concepts that can be illustrated by the five senses. If you are teaching that God gives us food, fill a basket with fruits, vegetables, and items from your pantry. Because these students are literal thinkers, use terms that will help them grasp the concept you want to convey. For example, "Jesus teaches His followers to share with their friends. Jesus tells us to let our friends play with our toys." "Jesus wants His followers to be honest. When your mother asks you if you broke the vase—and you did—say, 'yes.'"

3. Remember that these students need more time for learning. Repetition is the key to retention. Be patient and unhurried in teaching.

4. Use concise one- or two-step directions. Avoid time-consuming confusion by giving no more than two directions at a time.

5. Be sure the lesson is presented sequentially in small, easy-to-follow steps.

6. Make each lesson meaningful and applicable. Apply your lesson to everyday life and encourage all students to put what they have learned into practice.

Students With Learning Disabilities

1. Provide for needed breaks in concentration. Don't talk for extended periods. Break your schedule into segments so that the student is not expected to sit still and listen for long periods of time.

2. Continually refocus the student's attention. Use his name or touch him on his shoulder to draw his attention to you and the task at hand.

3. Reduce distracting noises and limit the visual environment behind you.

4. Use active learning strategies. Engaging in pencil-and-paper tasks only will be especially difficult for these students. Vary your approach by using clay, interest centers, games, music, drama, and other activities to heighten interest and involvement.

5. Be visually direct. Looking the student in the eye as you teach affirms the value you have placed on him as an individual.

6. Use multisensory teaching methods. Put the senses of sight, hearing, smell, taste, and touch to work as you make your lessons come alive.

7. Use motivational techniques. Watch all of your students and "catch them being good." Reward attentiveness and cooperation.

Students With Hearing Impairments

1. Do not shout!

2. If the child lip-reads, be sure he has a clear view of your mouth and face.

3. If the child wears hearing aids, be sure you have extra batteries on hand. Ask his parents to teach you how to adjust the aids and how to replace the batteries.

4. Provide a sign language interpreter, as necessary.

Students With Visual Impairments

1. Use clear, uncluttered visual aids.

2. Address the student by name. Give explanations each time an activity changes or when movement is necessary in the classroom.

3. Familiarize yourself with appropriate sighted-guide techniques (see page sixty-three). Ask the parents for guidance in training nondisabled students to be guides.

4. Explain guide-dog etiquette to your students if a dog will be attending class with their new classmate.

5. Provide braille or large-print materials. If you have purchased a student book for each student in your class, you do not need special permission to enlarge the pages of one book for your visually impaired student. Whenever you need more than one copy of a page, contact the publisher for special permission, unless the book is marked "reproducible."

Students With Physical Handicaps

1. Familiarize yourself with any special equipment, such as wheelchairs and/or braces. Help your students understand the use of this equipment and the need to respect and care for it.

2. Train student peers to assist with physical tasks beyond this student's capabilities.

3. If necessary, be sure your classroom is wheelchair accessible.

4. Obtain special supplies, such as double-handed scissors. These scissors, which allow a helper to hold the scissors along with the child, can be purchased through an office supply store.

Students With Speech Disorders

1. Develop a successful means of communicating with the child.

2. Never pretend to understand. Ask the child to repeat a statement or tell you in a different way. If you still cannot understand, ask the child to show you or to perhaps draw a picture to illustrate what is meant.

3. Give the child time to finish his statement. Don't do it for him.

Students With Emotional Disorders

1. Be loving, but firm.

2. Plan for success. This student may come to you with a negative self-image after repeated failures in other areas of his life. Encourage him with praise for even the smallest success, and provide opportunities for him to demonstrate his areas of competence.

3. Ask the student's parents to explain the behavioral interventions and discipline plan used at home and school. Implement the same interventions and plan in your classroom.

4. Being consistent applies not only to your management of behavior, but also to your response to the

child. For instance, be consistent with recognition, encouragement, and praise.

5. Don't make promises you can't keep. If you say you are going to give Jenny a call during the week—do it! Don't disappoint her.

INCLUDING THE TEENAGER

If your friend is a teenager, the following concepts will start the process of building friendships.

1. Teach teenagers to be buddies to their peers who have disabilities. Suggest specific ways to help: pushing a wheelchair, turning pages, assisting in feeding, or simply sitting with their friend during class or worship.

2. Study Jesus' interaction with people with disabilities. Let students list His responses (i.e., compassion, acceptance, touch). Study Scriptures such as Matthew 25:31-40 and Luke 14:7-24.

3. Hold a session in which teens will be introduced to the many careers open to them in Christian service in the disability community. Have information—or a representative—available from colleges that offer training in disability-related vocations.

4. Model Christlike responses to persons with disabilities. Because teens will learn by your example, it is important for you to lead out in displaying patience, compassion, and tolerance.

5. Invite an adult with a disability to visit your class or group. After a brief, informal presentation, allow students to ask questions.

6. Encourage teens to connect with community agencies that serve the disabled. Invite a representative of the Special Olympics to share with your students how they could be involved as coaches or assistants. Suggest that students volunteer for special programs offered through the local parks and recreation department.

7. Take time to prepare nondisabled students when you are aware that a teen with a disability will be joining your class. Give details about their new friend's disability, any specialized equipment he uses, and explain ways they can be his friend.

8. If you have a student with a disability and are unsure of his or her needs, ask.

9. Use simulation activities to help sensitize students to the daily struggles faced by those with disabilities. Lead a session in which each of your students has to perform a series of daily tasks while blindfolded, in a wheelchair, or physically limited in some other way. Spend time debriefing after this session.

INCLUDING THE ADULT

1. If the disability is mental retardation, you may want to have your adult Sunday school class sponsor a class for your friend. As a person ages, the social factors of the mental age become bigger components in this decision. Having such a class would provide an opportunity for residents of group homes, sheltered apartments, or other housing options to attend.

2. If your class does sponsor a separate class, be sure some time is arranged for the two groups to be together. Opening sessions, fellowship time, and social events can be great times for building bridges. During worship, arrange for class members to take turns sitting with the new members, assisting them in finding Scripture references, songs in the hymnal, taking Communion. Such an arrangement provides opportunities for mutual ministry and fellowship, fun at parties, and getting to know what nice people they really are. Adults with disabilities other than mental retardation can be a part of the regular Sunday school class.

3. If the disability is deafness, find a volunteer

interpreter to communicate the lesson. Ask the interpreter to conduct some basic sign language classes for class members.

4. If the disability is blindness, invite the prospective member to the class. Offer transportation. Orient the person to the classroom and the path he will take to get there. Ask class members not to move furniture or other objects without telling the blind person. Provide a braille Bible and other materials.

5. If the disability is the result of a stroke or other physical event, and the person has been a part of the class, keep him involved. Offer to provide transportation or assistance with other activities that would now be difficult for the person to handle independently. Even if communication is difficult, continue to try. Look the person in the eye. Make statements instead of asking questions. Visit the person at home. Let him know he is still an important part of the group. Make the building and the classroom accessible. When social activities are planned, consider the accessibility and overcome any barriers.

6. If the disability is emotional, be understanding and supportive. Ask the family or the person about the nature of the problem, the treatment, and what the class can do to help. Ask a mental-health professional to come to a class function and discuss the nature of mental illness.

7. If the disability is a learning disability, the teacher should consult students ahead of time before asking them to read aloud in class. Being cautious is all the more important with adults, since many adults have learning disabilities that have not been diagnosed.

Teaching the broad range of people with disabilities in the Sunday school is not difficult. It takes a friend to start the process, a church interested in the project, a class that wants real inclusion to happen, and a teacher who wants to make an eternal difference. In many cases, inclusion can result from a new "Well, why didn't I think of that!?" attitude.

I hope the result for you is what it was for me: a wonderful friend, a fellow Christian, plenty of good fruit, and the rehabilitation of a soul who just happened to live in a body with a disability.

ANOTHER REMARKABLE FRIEND

Her name is Jennifer. I didn't get to know Jennifer until after Helen's death. When I first met her, I noticed how much she reminded me of Helen. Like Helen, she has cerebral palsy. Like Helen, she works hard to communicate. Like Helen, she has a wonderful attitude. Like Helen, she has lots of friends. Like Helen, she is a committed Christian. Like Helen, she has her spiritual needs met by a caring congregation. But there is a difference, which we will talk about later.

Jennifer L. Heck was born in Louisville, Kentucky, on June 10, 1965. Brain damage was the result of a breech birth. Oxygen failed to reach the motor centers of her brain during several minutes of interrupted breathing. Although her parents suspected something was wrong in her development, it wasn't until Jennifer was fifteen months old that the doctors finally diagnosed her condition as cerebral palsy.

Even at this young age, the doctors could tell her case was mild, and told her family that with therapy and encouragement she could actually improve her ability. That's just what Mr. and Mrs. Heck did. They spent hours upon hours taking Jennifer to physical, speech, and occupational therapy at a nearby clinic, and then performing additional therapy at home. They also integrated her into "normal" relationships and activities with her three siblings.

For three years she attended a private school for

children with cerebral palsy. When it became apparent that her intellectual and emotional development were normal, her parents fought to get her into the public school system. She was granted permission, but remained in special education classes until the sixth grade. At this time Jennifer and her parents again fought for her to be mainstreamed into "regular" classes at Noe Middle School. There she served on the yearbook staff, received several academic awards, and blossomed in her social interactions.

Jennifer graduated from duPont Manual High School in 1983, in the top 5 percent of her class of four hundred students. During these four years, she was actively involved in the National Honor Society, student newspaper, and senior class leadership. She recalls the following highlights: making close friends for the first time in her life; becoming the senior class second vice-president after giving a campaign speech in front of four hundred classmates, in spite of her speech impediment; and getting her driver's license.

After high school, Jennifer went to Spalding University on a four-year scholarship. She made the dean's list several semesters, and was the editor-in-chief of the student newspaper for a year.

After two and a half years, she transferred to the University of Louisville. Within another two and a half years she graduated with a bachelor's degree in Business Administration, and earned a grade point average of 3.6. During her college years, Jennifer developed interpersonal skills through friendships and mandatory group work in classes. She received career guidance from professors and a business leader she met through a mentor program, and was involved with a campus ministry group that led her to rededicate her life to God and make Jesus Christ an integral part of her everyday living.

Realizing that she had no practical job experience and was getting nowhere with interviews, she decided to start her own computerized design company—Page Works. For two years she taught herself the skills in designing publications on a desktop computer system, making business contacts, and developing a portfolio of work experience. She was also involved in the American Business Women's Association.

It was through one of these contacts that she was offered a job. In June, 1990, she was hired by Goodwill Industries of Kentucky as a staff writer to produce the organization's newsletter. Within six months, she was hired full-time as a development specialist. She produced all of the organization's publications, maintained a mailing list of six thousand records, and supervised other public relations functions. She traveled around Kentucky conducting newsletter interviews and attended two seminars in Washington, DC, traveling alone. Jennifer was selected by her colleagues as "Employee of the Year" in 1991. Primarily because of her skills, Goodwill Industries won first place for "Outstanding Newsletter Award" for two consecutive years, and the "Outstanding Brochure Award" in 1992.

Since she was a teenager, Jennifer has dreamed of living on her own. Throughout college and after, she bought domestic furnishings in anticipation of the realization of her dream. Although her family was skeptical, on March 4, 1993, Jennifer moved into a new condo unit.

A few weeks after she bought her new home, Jennifer started contemplating what she wanted it to communicate to people who visited her, and to herself. Using wood contributed by an uncle, Jennifer and her father created a cross to hang above her mantle. The cross measures eighteen by twenty-four inches. A friend from Goodwill gave her a grapevine wreath, which became Christ's crown of thorns. This friend also helped her place three (symbolizing the

Trinity) clusters of green ivy (symbolizing Christ's everlasting life) and tiny white flowers (symbolizing Christ's purity and holiness) on the crown. Jennifer requested that a spotlight be installed over the fireplace, to shine down on the cross.

Both Helen and Jennifer lived at the peak of their abilities. Helen spent her life with her mother, who provided excellent care. Their lives were different, but fulfilled. The real difference between Helen and Jennifer is their ministry. Helen's relationship with the Lord led her to minister in her local church. Jennifer's relationship led her to serve the Lord as a full-time worker encouraging ministry for her companions who, like herself, have disabilities.

In April, 1996, Jennifer applied to enter Johnson Bible College. When accepted, she resigned her seven-year job as a graphic designer, sold her condo, and moved into a mobile home 250 miles from her security base of family, friends, and church.

She is working toward a second college degree with a minor in disability ministry. I am her advisor and friend. Her papers, even examinations, look like camera-ready publications. Her sparkling personality radiates her peace with her disability and her Lord. Even though her speech is difficult to understand and simple motor movements are a major chore, she is functional. She drives her car. She lives alone with some help. Daily routines are not easy. It takes her more than two hours to dress for the day.

It would be easy to give in to the disability, but Jennifer will not. Her vocational goal is to help people with disabilities find ministry. She resigned a good job, gave up a beautiful condo and other creature comforts, left a place in her congregation, and moved away from supportive parents to prepare herself for the task.

During a visit to my office, Jennifer expressed her appreciation for a statement I have on my office door. Written by John Wern, who is Director of Ministry with JAF Ministries, a disability ministry in California, the poignant sentence states: "Disability ministry is not disability ministry until the disabled are ministering." That sentence summarizes Jennifer's philosophy.

In her own words, she suggests four ways the church can assist people with disabilities to minister:

"DISABILITY MINISTRY IS NOT DISABILITY MINISTRY UNTIL THE DISABLED ARE MINISTERING."

1. Provide the transportation, if needed, to enable people with disabilities to be involved in the life of your church (i.e. worship, discipleship, fellowship and service opportunities).

2. Take time to know them as individuals. Find out their interests, abilities, activities in which they thrive, and their passions for service. If they can't verbalize these areas, observe them interacting with others and/or ask their parents, caregiver, or friends for insight.

3. Hook them up with a spiritual mentor who can guide them in discovering their gifts within the church community.

4. Rejoice in whatever way the Lord uses everyone to meet the needs of His people. God will bring glory to His holy name as all of His people work together in spreading His love and truth.

A favorite Scripture for Jennifer's philosophy is 1

Peter 4:10, 11: "Each one should use whatever gift he has received to serve others, faithfully administering God's grace in its various forms . . . so that in all things God may be praised through Jesus Christ. To him be the glory and the power for ever and ever. Amen."

Another item on my office wall says something about Jennifer. It is a poster made of eight pictures of Jennifer enjoying her hobby. The pictures were taken on Saturday, July 27, 1996, in Bardstown, Kentucky, where she made tandem skydives numbers four and five! I enjoy saying to Jennifer, "Until I learned what your hobby was, I didn't think the cerebral palsy had hurt your brain."

My two special friends with cerebral palsy illustrate two strong mission points: people with disabilities need to be included in the educational programs of the church, and people with disabilities need to minister.

-----

[1]Peggy DaHarb, comp. *Tips for Teachers, Early Childhood;*
Dianna Golata and Nancy Karpenske, comp. *Tips for Teachers, Elementary;*
Kim Jackson, comp. *Tips for Teachers, Teens;*
Brett DeYoung, comp. *Tips for Teachers, Adults,* Cincinnati: Standard Publishing Co., 1995.

CHAPTER 7

A CARING, RESPONSIVE CONGREGATION

His name is Charles. Among my friends with disabilities, I have never known another with as much wrong with him as Charles. Born December 15, 1961, Charles Combs was not a typical, bouncing baby boy. He was born with Down syndrome. In addition, his first vertebra was unstable, which made it appear that he did not have a neck. He was a dwarf, had some brain damage, was blind in the left eye, and had a deformed left hip and knee. After birth he developed diabetes and became insulin dependent, developed cirrhosis of the liver from hepatitis B, and had surgery to correct some urinary difficulties. With so much wrong with him, it is little wonder his doctors told his parents he would not live past his ninth birthday.

When I first met him, he was in his mid-twenties, seated in a wheelchair. I noticed some features of Down syndrome, his short stature, and some speech problems. After talking with his parents, Mary and Virgil, I got a longer list of his physical disabilities. At this time, Charles was in a pattern of going into the hospital to get units of blood because of bleeding around the surgery site. Often he would require as much as four units of blood.

His parents provided exceptional care for their son. In order to hear changes in his breathing and be aware when he would start bleeding, Mary slept in his room. Although not a nurse, she was skilled at what she needed to do for her son. Virgil was understanding of her attention to their firstborn and assisted her in the difficult routines.

Virgil and Mary experienced a particularly tough time during the two years Charles lived in an institution. They hadn't wanted to make the placement, but thought the doctor's advice was right. However, they agonized everytime they took Charles back after vacations. Finally, they decided to keep him at home. He was home for a holiday break when the decision was made: Charles would not return to the facility. Virgil said, "We don't have all of his clothing." Mary replied, "That's OK. I will make him new clothes and go to garage sales." He never left them again.

Beloved by other church members, Charles was a true member; he participated, he was included.

Charles returned to his community. He led a full life. He enjoyed attending school, especially riding the "little yellow bus." In addition, he participated in a sheltered workshop program. In general, he became a well-known figure around town.

A big part of his community life was his church. When Charles's body grew bigger than the others in the Beginner Class, the teacher made him her assistant so that he would have a reason to stay and hear the stories of Jesus' life. He sang and signed solos when he attended church camp. Beloved by other church members, Charles was a true member; he participated, he was included.

My friendship with Charles started when I visited his church because the members had sent money to support the ministries of the Foundation. I was drawn to Charles and his family. On one visit I had lunch at their house. At every visit, I saw Charles's wonderful smile as he flitted about in his wheelchair speaking to friends and sharing his love for them. Every visit except the last.

On this visit there was no Charles when I arrived at the church. His father explained that because Charles's health had deteriorated, he was in the hospital in Dayton. He said that Charles would like to see me and asked if I had time to visit him. I replied, "Of course I have time to see my friend."

Before I went to the airport, we drove to the hospital. The prognosis was right. Charles did not look good. When he saw me he managed a faint grin, and addressed me as "Im." I hugged him and visited for a while. When he told me that he was tired and wanted "me [go] Jesus oooh shoot," I didn't understand the meaning. His mother explained that watching cowboy and Indian movies had influenced his concept of death. Death meant being shot by a gun. When Charles said, "Oooh shoot," he was saying he wanted to go be with his Lord. I will always remember our last embrace. I had to work to get my arms through tubes and wires of the machines hooked to him. I realized I

AT EVERY VISIT, I SAW CHARLES'S WONDERFUL SMILE AS HE FLITTED ABOUT IN HIS WHEELCHAIR SPEAKING TO FRIENDS AND SHARING HIS LOVE FOR THEM.

would not see him again on this earth. I told his parents to let me know when there was a change. They remembered my request.

When I returned home from a speaking trip on a Sunday night, the message from Mary on the answering machine was, "Charles is about ready to receive his angel wings." I called immediately. The report was, "Jim, he died about two hours ago. We had removed all of the tubes and wires. He wanted to die at home. I was holding him in my arms and his last words sounded like 'Home, home.'" He was now in his heavenly home.

Following Charles's death, his parents donated his battery-powered wheelchair to the Christian Church Foundation for the Handicapped. In a few weeks, the program director of the Ebenezer Christian Community, which the Foundation administers in Mexico, informed me that three children with severe physical problems were being admitted. She needed wheelchairs. Charles' chair was sent. After being adapted to Ricky's needs, it is now in good use. I can see Charles's smile and imagine him saying, "Good, Im."

PROMOTING CONGREGATION AWARENESS

Charles was a part of a caring, responsive congregation. His church wanted to include him and to meet his spiritual needs. Before discussing what you can do to help your congregation include your friend, let's look at how congregations across America are doing with inclusion.

Early on, the typical approach was to sign services for persons who were deaf and start special Sunday school classes for persons with mental retardation. Today, the approach is more eclectic. All disability groups are included, and inclusion is emphasized. Many church groups have become involved with the spiritual development of members with disabilities.

How are the churches doing? The anecdotal evidence is mixed. Some families say their congregations have nothing to offer their child with a disability. Other families report that their congregations are doing a great job meeting their spiritual needs and those of their children.

A recent Louis Harris poll reported that 36 percent of Americans with disabilities attend religious services at least once a week, and 49 percent attend at least once a month. These attendance levels are just a little lower than among adults without disabilities, 58 percent of whom attend religious services at least once a month.[1] From some unknown source, I have often quoted the statistic that only 5 percent of persons with disabilities have a relationship with the church. The Harris poll seems to suggest this situation is improving. Reports of churches opening their programs to persons with disabilities are increasing. It is a trend that will continue.

THE ANSWER to full inclusion is for each church member to make a person with a disability a part of his life.

Interestingly, the answer to full inclusion in the church is to provide each church member with the information that will assist him in making the person with a disability a part of his life. The one-on-one approach is effective.

The following information will give you some pointers on how to start the process of making your congregation aware of your friend's spiritual needs.

STEP ONE

Learn what your friend's spiritual awareness and needs are. Discuss your faith and your church with your friend and his family. Does he go to church? Does his family? Does he understand religious concepts such as God, Jesus, prayer?

STEP
TWO

Tell your pastor that you have found a friend with a disability and you would like him to be a part of the life of your congregation. Briefly, describe the nature of the disability, how your friend learns, his social situation, and how much he already understands about church.

The minister needs to be reminded that people with disabilities have spiritual natures—as all of us have. Sometimes, even Christian, professionals in the disability community overlook the need for spiritual nurture. A veteran manager of a group home for adults with mental retardation responded after a speech I made on the necessity of opening the church to the disability community by saying, "I knew they *liked* to go to church but it never occurred to me they *should*. Because they are 'special,' I thought God would take care of things." This is a common belief and attitude. We are all "special." Your minister should know that 85 percent of persons with mental retardation can learn on an adult level. The important factor in learning and functioning is mental age.

Share the following statistics with your minister:

- Four out of five marriages that either produce a child with a disability or include a spouse who becomes disabled through accident or disease will end in divorce.
- Children with cognitive problems are subject to abuse ten times more than typical children.
- The incidence of abuse in families with a disabled child is twice that of typical families.
- Nine out of ten women who find through amniocentesis that their unborn child has Down syndrome choose to abort.
- Siblings of a child with a disability are four times more likely to be maladjusted than their peers who have typical siblings.

Suggest that a simple survey be put in a church publication, which will locate people with disabilities and families already associated with your congregation who need ministry. In the survey, define clearly what is meant by disability. Listing the types of disabilities will help: mental retardation, autism, Down syndrome, mental illness, cerebral palsy, spina bifida, blindness, deafness, etc. In this survey you will want to convey your interest in people with disabilities and your desire to minister to them.

Recommend that the church host a disability awareness Sunday or weekend. Such an event will enable members to:

- know more about people with disabilities
- be more sensitive to their needs
- know that their spiritual needs are as important as those of typical people
- be motivated to include them
- know that the most important part of the person is his soul

Suggest that the event have the following components:

- **A theme.** "The Variety in Ability." "Christ's Love Is Inclusive and Accessible."
- **A sermon.** Using a Scripture event describing Jesus' encounter with disability is always good. It gives a Biblical foundation for the outreach.
- **Music.** Using any of the thousands of hymns written by Fanny Crosby will speak to the value of people with disabilities using their talents in the church. (Fanny Crosby was blind from the age of six weeks.)
- **Special Music.** There are many possibilities, but my favorite is, "Sometimes Miracles Hide" (Word, 1991). My favorite soloist is Danna Delafield, a

mother of a son with Down syndrome. At the conclusion of her song, David will often walk onstage and help his mom finish the song. (I tell more of David's story in the afterword of this book.)

• **A Testimony.** Having a family tell of the importance of developing faith in their child helps the congregation see that all Christian parents treasure faith and want their children to have it.

• **Personnel With Disabilities.** Use people with disabilities to serve as ushers, sing, play an instrument, read Scripture.

• **Bulletin Cover.** Use a bulletin cover that stresses the theme and purpose of the day.

• **Sunday School.** Have every teacher in the Sunday school department teach the same lesson. Using a story from Jesus' ministry can be applied to all age groups.

• **Follow-Up.** Your disability awareness weekend will generate many good intentions. Capture them. Use a survey to identify needs in the church family and the members who are willing to be involved in meeting those needs.

• **Ideas.** Have a member of the congregation spend the day in a wheelchair, another blindfolded, another with both hands bandaged, and another wearing earplugs. At some point, having them report their experiences will help everyone to have some indication of how disability feels.

• **A list of resources.** The following organizations can offer some help:

JAF Ministries
   PO Box 3333, Agoura Hills, California 91301
Christian Church Foundation for the Handicapped
   PO Box 9869, Knoxville, Tennessee 37940

STEP THREE   If the minister suggests that you present the idea to the board or a committee, do so, using the same approach you used with him.

Talk up the idea in your Sunday school class or other small group. Share the positive experience you are having with your friend with a disability. Bring your friend to class. Encourage your fellow church members to befriend a person with a disability.

STEP FOUR

Organize a disability ministry team task force to analyze the results of the survey. Put into place the programs that will accommodate the spiritual needs of the people already associated in some way.

STEP FIVE

Continue to enjoy your friend as you watch his spiritual development. For example, for several months I observed Pat, a young lady with severe mental retardation, being taught stories about the life of Jesus. Every Sunday a new visual was constructed to illustrate the lesson. Discouraged by the lack of response from her pupil, the teacher asked if she should continue her lessons. I urged her to continue and agreed to visit the class the next Sunday.

STEP SIX

The lesson that day, based on Jesus' healing of Peter's mother-in-law, was dramatized with clothespins. Following the lesson, I asked Pat what the lesson was about. Pat laid the clothespin representing Peter's mother-in-law on the table. Slowly, she "walked" Jesus over to the mother-in-law. She leaned Jesus toward the mother-in-law until the clothespins touched. Popping her lips to indicate that Jesus had kissed her, Pat stood the mother-in-law upright. I was holding the clothespin representing Peter. Pat grunted and punched me to get Peter to join in the dancing around the table. When I asked her who made the mother-in-law well, she responded verbally (a rarity for her), "Jesus."

Spiritual development can happen at any emotional/intellectual/physical stage if the person is placed in a warm, open, responsive congregation. Try it; your friend will appreciate your efforts.

CHRISTIAN HOPE: A FINE EXAMPLE
OF AN INVOLVED CONGREGATION

"We need your help with a little boy who comes to our church," was the opening sentence of a telephone conversation with Larry Woodley, minister of the Christian Hope Church of Christ in Plymouth, North Carolina. My former student and dear friend was inviting me to conduct some workshops on how the congregation could meet the needs of people with disabilities. I was impressed that a congregation of about one hundred people would fly in a consultant to meet the needs of one child. During this telephone visit he repeated a theme, "We have got to help this family." Larry's good heart represented the heart of the congregation as well. After some discussion, we worked out a date.

"WE NEED YOUR HELP WITH A LITTLE BOY WHO COMES TO OUR CHURCH. WE HAVE GOT TO HELP THIS FAMILY."

The date arrived and so did a storm over the airport at Kinston, just as we were ready to land. To make up for the hour lost in circling the airport, Larry (without a valid pilot's license), flew across coastal North Carolina in his Lincoln Town Car to make it to the church on time for the first session of the weekend of activities. From this first visit I liked the place. Actually, I loved the people. They were friendly, the Eastern Carolina cuisine was deliciously different to my Eastern Tennessee palate (especially their kind of barbecue, and collards with corn-meal dumplings), and the congregation had a sincere interest in people with disabilities. Their concern this weekend was for young Chris Rhodes, whose severe seizures made public education difficult even in special placements.

During the weekend of instruction, I recommended a plan that provided a two-hour program on Sunday morning to accommodate Chris and his parents. For that time period the teachers provided music, lessons on his level, a comfortable place to recline after a seizure (which happened often), and supervision to allow his parents to be together in worship. Marie Ange, Melba Styons, and Emma Browning have been faithful to Chris. Miss Marie, Miss Melba, and Miss Emma (salutations in keeping with the locale), often give reports of how much it means to them to work with Chris. In their enthusiasm, they sound as though they are receiving the service, not giving it.

The key factor in a congregation's concern for people with disabilities is its minister. In short, the minister is the pacesetter. Larry Woodley serves as an excellent example of this principle. I met him in the courses I taught in English Grammar and Composition and Public Speaking at Johnson Bible College. Larry was an older student in my classes who didn't recall a lot about gerunds and adverbs. I admire older students who return to the academic world years after graduating from high school. Larry and I shared a mutual admiration for each other. His straight forwardness, good humor, and dedication were all traits I like in a person. One of the toughest events we shared was the stillbirth of the Woodley's second child. They asked me to do the funeral.

Since that first consultation in 1978, the congregation has been faithful to Chris. A classroom was assigned. When all of the other classrooms were given a plaque designating their use, Chris's door was labeled *Special Education*.

The faithfulness of the congregation is coupled with a special brand of loving encouragement. For example, Christian Hope has a practice of presenting a book to each of its high school graduates. The Sunday after the annual event was held, Larry telephoned me a bit guilt-stricken: Chris, who would have graduated that year if he hadn't had so much to cope with, had not been included. The problem was solved quickly. The next Sunday, June 9, 1996, was dubbed "Chris Rhodes Day." Wanda and Carroll, Chris's parents, sat up front with their son. Larry commended their faith in God and their parenting skills with their son. He also praised the congregation for their response to Chris and his family. The Rhodes family was presented an inspirational book. My wife and I liked the idea so much we sent flowers for the occasion. A special notice in the church bulletin captured the purpose of the day. "In Honor and Recognition of Chris Rhodes: If Chris had not been [disabled], he would have graduated this past week with Stephanie and Brad. In recognizing Chris, we also must give recognition to his family, Carroll and Wanda, whose dedication and perseverance have been an example to us all. They have brought Chris to church regularly when it probably would have been so much easier to have stayed at home. We know that their efforts have not gone unnoticed by our wonderful Lord."

Over the years, Chris's parents and I have become warm friends. Chris is now a young adult, and he continues to have special needs, but they will be met, faithfully and lovingly, by the members of Christian Hope.

> THE FAITHFULNESS
> *of the congregation
> is coupled with
> a special brand
> of loving
> encouragement.*

The Christian Hope attitude shows in its architecture. My first visit was to a white frame structure about ten miles from downtown Plymouth. Today, the refurbished brick building boasts nine classrooms and a fellowship hall. The building has a well-designed access ramp and two shortened benches to provide floor space for wheelchairs.

The way the members feel about people with disabilities is also reflected in their missions outreach. The congregation is a generous supporter of the Christian Church Foundation for the Handicapped. In addition to sending a monthly check, they visit, write notes, send special donations. Mrs. Hilda Hardison, a lovely lady, is the liaison between the ministry and the congregation. When I see her, "Miss Hilda" asks me about events and situations. As director of the Foundation I have to work to remember the details—because she remembers everything!

The most recent example of Christian Hope's level of concern occurred when word was received that Wendy and Derek Roberson's four-month-old son, Kolby, had been diagnosed with spinal muscular atrophy. The first Sunday after the news was known, Larry's morning sermon addressed the issue of suffering, the sufficiency of God's grace, and God's love and purpose for His children. His compassion was clear, even on the tape that I reviewed. The conclusion of the sermon offered suggestions for the members to support the family. In candor, Larry stated that Kolby was dying. The diagnosis had been confirmed. He asked the members not to say, "I know how you feel." Rather, Christian Hope's caring people were encouraged to embrace, be available, listen, and meet practical needs.

> INSTEAD OF saying, "I know how you feel," embrace, be available, listen, and meet practical needs.

The emotional and spiritual support for the family was immediate. Church members were available on frequent hospitalizations, they went by to check on Kolby and his family, and regular reports were made to the congregation. When Larry and I visited the house, Wendy reported to me in awe that Miss Hardison, one of the beloved saints of the congregation, had played with Wendy's children on the floor.

When I ask Larry to explain the Christian Hope approach to people with disabilities, he never varies his response: "We just try to meet people's needs." One night Larry, Fran, and I were driving from the church to their house. The conversation turned to a family in the community who was experiencing some difficulty. Fran said to Larry, "We have got to see what we can do to help them." Larry replied, "Yes, I'll take care of that tomorrow." I don't know what he did, but I know the minister. If the resources were not immediately available, he called someone and said, "We have a family in our church who needs your kind of help. Will you come and help us help them?"

---

[1]National Organization on Disability. *Closing the Gap. The N.O.D./Harris Survey of Americans With Disabilities—A Summary.* Washington, DC., 1994, page 25.

CHAPTER 8

COPING WITH
A LEARNING DISABILITY

His name is Chris. When I first knew him he was five years old. He was a taller-than-average, well-proportioned, handsome boy. The occupational therapy department at the children's rehabilitation center I directed provided an excellent service to young children with learning disabilities. Many children were helped. Chris Lape was one of them. Following a thorough evaluation of Chris's abilities for sensory integration, he was placed in a remedial program that addressed his specific area of deficiency.

Chris moved to Knoxville with his family in 1975. His father, an army major, was sent by the army to the University of Tennessee to study for a master's degree in civil engineering and then to teach in the ROTC department. Prior to the move, Chris's parents knew there were developmental problems but couldn't get anyone, especially anyone in the medical community, to provide a diagnosis or offer help. Finally, at five years of age, Chris was diagnosed with minimal brain dysfunction and hyperactivity. Today, his problem would be called a learning disability.

When he enrolled in the public school system, Chris was referred to the sensory integration program at our center. He attended twice a week for two years. Testing revealed a rather severe problem. He still had primitive reflexes. The worst was the tilting reaction. When he was on all fours and his hand was pulled to the right, his head would follow. Typically the reflex disappears by the time a child is six to eight months old. Chris was over sixty months.

A pesky reflex wasn't his only problem. He had to learn to put his right hand on his left ear. Any hand movement stopped in the middle of his body. If sitting at a table to color a picture, he would color the left half of the picture with his left hand, put the crayon in his right hand and color the right half of the page. If he crawled into a play tunnel with both ends open, he couldn't determine how to get himself out.

Chris remembers the negative feelings, embarrassment, and frustration he experienced by being unable to tie his shoes as a second grader, or to tell time as a third grader. Having to ask for help with his shoes and ask the time from age-mates did not add to the self-esteem of an already frustrated child.

According to Chris's assessment, elementary school was "tough." During those years he remembers tutors who helped him with motor skills and balance. He recalls flash cards to teach colors and to help him with spelling.

In conjunction with the programs at the rehabilitation center and the school, he was enrolled in a biofeedback program aimed at helping him learn to relax when he felt the hyperactivity increasing and to reduce his need for Ritalin. He learned to relax. His parents did exercises at home. Schoolteachers would help. One teacher arranged a system with Chris. When she saw he was getting uptight, she would lay her hand on his shoulder to remind him to do his relaxation exercises.

Even though Chris was the youngest person in his

group, he benefited the most from the experience. He was actually able to stop taking the Ritalin. Chris still uses the relaxation techniques he learned in that program and probably will for the rest of his life.

Middle school years were somewhat easier, but eighth grade got harder again. High school, according to Chris, "didn't get any easier" and according to his mother it was "terrible." He flunked science and algebra and had to retake the courses. Frustration and not being able to concentrate were hallmarks of his high school days.

His family helped. Because his older brother was an A and B student, Chris believed his parents expected him to do the same. For four years his parents encouraged him to try harder and told him he could do it. Chris says that the best help he received in his struggle with learning disability was from his parents. They encouraged him to set the tone for his life, assisted with skills to cope with his learning disability, told him he was responsible, and helped him with his homework. While he assigns his parents the number-one slot of the best help to him, he is quick to add, "I can't leave God out of the equation. I would pray, 'God help me. I want to learn, but I don't know what to do.'"

DEFYING *the assertions that he should learn a trade, he graduated from college!*

His learning problems were only a part of the frustration of high school. He developed mononucleosis. Chris confesses, "In high school I didn't know how to study, and I guess the reason no one helped me was that they didn't understand how my brain worked."

Sometime during his junior year, something clicked. Chris describes his feelings, "I was in Nowheresville." Guidance counselors had led him to believe that his choices for a vocation were limited;

he could learn a trade or join the army. Chris decided he would make himself learn—and he did! He found that highlighting important passages helped him retain the material. He added other techniques to help himself learn. He graduated from high school.

Motivation appeared. He felt God calling him to work with young people. He reasoned that if he was to be a youth minister, he had to have a degree from college.

With highlighter in hand, he enrolled at Johnson Bible College. The first two years weren't good; he burned out. Because he dropped out for one semester, college was a five-year adventure. He worked. He prayed. His parents encouraged. He prayed. His friends encouraged. His senior year was his best—a 3.3 grade point! Defying the assertions that he would never go to college and should learn a trade, he graduated from college!

CHRIS DECIDED HE WOULD MAKE HIMSELF LEARN—AND, USING A HIGHLIGHTER, HE DID!

Because of my contact with Chris at church, I knew that his high school and college years had been difficult. Then one Sunday, Chris was scheduled to speak about his summer plans at our church. When he was introduced, a tall, handsome young man stood up and walked gracefully to the speaker's stand. Where, I wondered, was the little boy who had a positive primitive reflex at age five?

He told us about Missionary Athletes International, a Christian organization that spreads the gospel through athletics. Chris explained that he would work in soccer camps in England, training young children in the sport, while also teaching them about Jesus through Bible lessons, songs, testimonies, and prayer. For a week in Spain and one in Portugal, the team of athletes would play local and professional soccer teams. Was this the young man who had to have speech therapy and couldn't find his way out of a play tunnel? I was moved to tears.

As many as 15 percent of the young people he has worked with as a youth minister have learning disabilities.

When he was ordained as a youth minister, he asked me to pray. I thanked God: "We are grateful for all the factors that have brought Chris to this day. We are grateful for godly parents who have reared him in Your ways. We are grateful for Jim and Mary's concern about a developmental problem in their young son that led them to seek help. Because of Your grace and provision, Chris has overcome the problem, and this weekend has received a college degree which will enhance his ministry for You."

How are things with Chris today? He reports, "I still struggle with the LD. My attention span is a problem. I still 'clue out.' In conversations I often ask, 'Will you say that again?'"

As many as 15 percent of the young people he has worked with as a youth minister have learning disabilities. His approach is to help them focus, set goals, and consider what is important. Parents are inspired by his example. When he reveals that he has overcome a learning disability, parents cannot believe it. He reminds them that his parents were told he would never graduate from college and that he would have to learn a trade. He focused on being a youth minister and got the degree his professional choice demanded.

How does he see his future? Chris believes he could get his master's degree. He would have to do a lot of highlighting, but he could do it. If he decided to change professions, and get a degree in history and a teacher's certificate, he could do it. Then this winner added, "Ministry gives me the greatest pleasure. I don't need to be in a big church with hundreds of people. Ministry to me is making an impact on people's lives, one at a time."

His wife, Lorie, is a nurse. She has brought special joy to Chris. His technique for overcoming his learning disability also works in his marriage. Hubby reports, "When we read marriage books, Lorie just reads them and understands them—I have to use my highlighter!"

Today, Chris is doing what he wants to do. He is organized, has direction, loves to reach kids for God, and does thoughtful deeds. For example, he sends tapes of his sermons to his parents. They don't remember hearing a single one that didn't express appreciation to them for what they have done for him.

HELPING A FRIEND
WHO HAS A LEARNING DISABILITY

In recent times, people with learning disabilities have generated a lot of interest among people in the school system, the college world, medicine, and the media. This interest is due in part to the dramatic increase in the number of people with learning disabilities. Some of this increase is the result of a change in definition and better diagnostic techniques, but there does appear to be more people in the group. Children with learning disabilities are the largest group receiving special education services in the school system. Students with learning disabilities make up the largest disability group enrolling in college. Physicians are diagnosing more people with "Attention Deficit Syndrome" and "Attention Deficit Syndrome with Hyperactivity Disorder." People in both of these categories may have a learning disability as a symptom. The media reports on the wide use of Ritalin to control the problems. So, if your friend has a learning disability, he is in a large group. "He" is the correct pronoun because more than 72 percent of persons with learning disabilities are male. Any culture, race, nationality, or language group will have people with learning disabilities.

People with learning disabilities have normal and above IQs. As a matter of fact, there is a subgroup titled, "Gifted-Learning Disabled." People in this group will have academic problems; the two major ones are reading and mathematics. Probably, the group most widely known are those with dyslexia, which means the person cannot read because they cannot correctly interpret writing symbols. The problem is caused by a slight brain dysfunction. Lack of oxygen at birth is a frequently reported cause.

While I have defined what a learning disability is, the most useful information is to know what the person deals with. Whatever the cause, neurological damage will always be there. The person with the learning problems will have to learn to cope or use medicine to control the feelings resulting from it.

If I were a child with a learning disability, here is what I would want you to know about me:
- I am trying to sit still.
- I can't keep my mind on one subject very long.
- A noise outside will distract me.
- I don't always pick up on clues about how you are feeling.

- I can be impulsive.
- Often I do something and then think about it.
- I try to listen, but my mind wanders.
- I know that I don't read well.
- I don't always remember.
- I lose my belongings.
- In my mind one and one do not always equal two.
- Often I feel stupid.
- I am really a nice person, struggling with not being able to learn and stay focused.

If your friend is being included in Sunday school, the teacher can make the learning easier if she implements these ideas:

- Create a classroom of caring people for the child.
- Make every member of the class feel competent.
- Provide a peer tutor, buddy, or just a friend to help in the classroom.
- Change the pace to alter the concentration.
- Give directions slowly and one at a time.
- Don't distribute materials until they are needed.
- Vary the activities.
- Be sure the child with the learning problem is listening.
- Praise every student, but look for reasons to praise the child with the learning disability.
- Be sure the child knows he is surrounded by God's love.

If your friend is an adult, talk to him about how he is affected by his learning disability. Knowing his needs will help build your friendship. For example, my friend Chris confesses that he still "clues out." (I like that expression!) When your friend "clues out," don't be offended or frustrated—that only adds to the problem. Be understanding and ask, "Where were we in our conversation when you clued out?" If you notice that your friend is fidgety, suggest a walk, or at least move around.

If the adult friend is in a Sunday school class, let the teacher know that calling on him to read or having the class read consecutive verses in turn could be a disaster. The teacher should ask your friend privately if he would like to read before calling on him. Also, asking the person a direct question may be embarrassing if he is in the middle of not being able to concentrate.

Help your friend find his "highlighter"—ways to overcome his learning disability. Help him find confidence in knowing he is unconditionally loved by God and you.

CHAPTER 9

PATIENCE MAY OPEN THE DOOR TO AUTISM

His name is Casey. Once when my wife and I were out driving, we passed a car whose model or make we didn't know. I asked, "Where is Casey when we need him?"

Casey has autism. Like many who have autism (pervasive developmental disorder), Casey has an incredible ability; he knows the make and model of any car he sees.

I have known Casey's family for years. His grandparents on both sides, and most of his aunts and uncles, have attended or are otherwise associated with Johnson Bible College, so I have friendly feelings for both families. When Jody Rood, from the paternal side, married Penny Baker, from the maternal side, the marriage was a nice blending of the two families.

Casey's family attends the same church we do, so we heard the good news of Penny's pregnancy; the Roods were going to have twins. A few weeks later the prayer chain was activated. One of the twins was in trouble and later died before birth. Nothing would be done about Jesse's body until Casey had developed enough to be viable. When Casey was born, it was a sad/happy time. Sad because there was a funeral for Jesse; happy for Casey's safe arrival.

As Casey matured, it was obvious that his developmental milestones were not typical. The teachers who worked with Casey in Sunday school and children's church often had a variety of conversations about him, which centered around topics like: "What is the matter with Casey?" "Why does he act that way?" "All he wants to do is read a book." "He can tell you the name of any car."

I arranged a time with the director of children's services to observe him; she and I agreed that there was a problem. One of her comments was that he could be given a book and he would be happy for hours. After I observed him, I talked with his parents. They didn't express this thought, but I felt that their reaction was a mixture of relief and appreciation that someone was concerned. As is often the case, the parents had different fixes on what the situation was. Mom, because she "just felt" there was a problem, had read a lot. Her conclusion was autism. Dad was more pragmatic. He knew there was a problem, but believed Casey would outgrow it. During our chat, I learned that Casey's pediatrician probably had thought there was a problem but just hadn't said it. The result of our meeting was that I would arrange

CASEY HAS AN INCREDIBLE ABILITY; HE KNOWS THE MAKE AND MODEL OF ANY CAR HE SEES.

to have Casey tested by therapists in the school system and, if necessary, place him in an appropriate program.

The testing suggested autism, and Casey was placed in an excellent preschool program. The calls I made to the supervisor of the program let me know Casey was making progress, but one day I decided I wanted to see firsthand how my little friend was doing. With his parents' permission, I went to the school. I arrived at music time.

As I entered the room, I noticed a recently polished, older model car parked outside the classroom window. When Casey saw me, I got a typical autistic reaction; he knew I was there but he didn't look at me. The music on the recorder was lively.

> IT HAS BEEN *wonderful watching Casey develop and be a part of his world, especially his church.*

The music therapist insisted I participate. I did. Afterwards I sat in a child-size chair to study Casey's interactions. I was pleased. I felt good inside. I thought, *He is getting the help he needs. His grandparents, both bunches, will be happy. We need to include him in programs at the church.*

My pleasant thoughts were interrupted when I realized Casey was walking backwards toward me. I thought he would stop, but he kept coming. I opened my arms and enfolded him with a hug. He knew he was with his friend. Then it happened. With his head he gestured toward the car outside the window and reported: "1967 Pontiac."

It has been wonderful watching Casey develop and be a part of his world, especially his church. After a children's day event at the art museum in our town, my wife and I stopped for lunch with our grandsons at a fast-food restaurant. Because the boys wanted to eat outside (really they wanted to play on the playground), we went outside. Casey, one of his brothers, and his father, had made the same restaurant choice. As we supervised the children, who were playing more than eating, Sean, my youngest grandson, yelled, "Hey, Casey, come here and try this!" Casey and Sean are in the same Sunday school class. They are friends. They know each other's names.

BEFRIENDING A PERSON WITH AUTISM

You can guide your friend with autism to be included in the life of your church. While I am happy with Casey's general progress, I am most pleased with his spiritual development. In Sunday school he is no longer isolated from his peers nor does he occupy his time with a book. He sits at the table and learns the stories about Jesus and His purpose for coming to earth. Casey knows he is one of the reasons Jesus came. Your friend is another.

When I was a student, and even as a college teacher, I was told, have read, and taught that autism is a rare disorder. The statistics then were four in every ten thousand births. I am not sure of this figure anymore. I would agree with more recent information, which suggests ten to fifteen per ten thousand births. Anecdotal evidence also suggests that there are more cases of autism than previously existed. Teacher friends of mine tell me so. One preschool special education teacher in a metropolitan area told me that in three previous years her staff had not worked with one child with Down syndrome, but in just one year they had three children with autism. At a Christian education conference, the children's director of a large congregation reported several children with autism in her groups. The point of this information is that the church is more likely than ever to encounter a youngster with autism.

Understanding autism will help with the inclusion process in your church. Probably the most widely accepted definition of autism is the one used by the IDEA: "a developmental disability significantly affecting verbal and nonverbal communication and social interaction, usually evident before age three, that adversely affects a child's educational performance." Other characteristics often associated with autism are:

- engagement in repetitive activities and stereotyped movements
- resistance to environmental change or change in daily routines
- unusual responses to sensory experiences.

That's the textbook definition; here is what you will see:

Likely the most noticeable characteristic is difficult communication. The child may not speak, may have limited use of language, may use repetitive phrases, or carry on a non-typical conversation. Abstract concepts will give him trouble.

MORE RECENT information suggests ten to fifteen cases of autism per ten thousand births.

The child will not relate well to people, events, or objects. Often the child with autism will avoid eye contact. For instance, you and the child may be the only people in the room, but you will know he isn't looking at you. Events and objects, unless it is an object he likes, will be equally detached from his attention.

Next, the child will play for long periods of time. Interest in one toy or object is common. A book, a spoon, a favorite toy will occupy the child's attention for hours.

Further, environmental change is difficult for the child with autism. Any change in schedule—how silverware is placed on the table, which sweater he wears—will get a reaction, often a loud one.

Then, the child with autism will have unusual responses to sensory information. Loud noises, lights, textures of food, the fabric of his clothes, all will receive marked attention.

Finally, repetitive body movements and behavior patterns are common. He will flap his hands, or flip his fingers in front of his eyes, or develop some similar motion.

The child with autism will display many of the following characteristics in an educational setting, public school, or Sunday school. Alicia Lauvray, a student of mine, adapted this chart, which gives a graphic look at the behavior of a child with autism.

Signs and Symptoms of Autism

1. Has difficulty mixing with other children.

2. Acts deaf.

3. Resists learning.

4. Has no fear of real dangers.

5. Giggles and laughs inappropriately.

6. Is markedly overactive or underactive.

It is important for you to know your friend with autism. I suggest that you make two visits, one to his home and one to his school.

At his house, notice his behavior. How does he interact with family members, his toys, and his environment? Ask his parents if he has an unusual attachment to something. It could be crayons, a book, a piece of string. Ask what sensory experience causes the child to react: a light being turned on, a sudden noise. Learn what his eating habits are. Children with autism often prefer one food and are bothered by a certain texture of food. Assure the family

7. Resists change in routine.

8. Indicates needs by gesture.

9. Is not cuddly.

10. Avoids eye contact.

11. Manifests inappropriate attachment to objects.

12. Spins objects.

13. Plays intently for abnormally long periods.

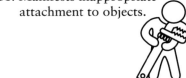

14. Has standoffish manner.

of your concern for them and their child.

At his school, watch the techniques teachers use. Note especially the behavior control methods they use. Because of confidentiality, the parents or guardian will have to give permission for you to visit. If it can be arranged, the time will be well worth the effort.

The more you know about your friend, the easier it will be for you to relate to him and him to you.

Following these visits, take the child on some outings. The options are many. If you have children, include your new friend in family trips to the zoo, a movie, a walk in the park, a trip to the playground, or to the ice cream store. If you don't have children, take the child on your own or include other children the age of your little friend.

If your friend with autism is an adult, follow a similar procedure. Visit his home, group home, sheltered apartment, or wherever he lives. The living situation will give you some insight into the person's ability. Going to his place of employment will add further insight. The more you know about your friend, the easier it will become for you to relate to him and him to you. Time and patience are the watchwords.

Since our focus is to get the person into a Christian education program, let's work on a plan to make that happen. Set a goal: "In three months my friend with autism will be included in a Bible school class with his peers."

STEP
ONE

Arrange a meeting with the family, a member of the church staff, the teacher of the class in question, and a parent of a child without a disability, to discuss the plans for including the person in the class. An important part of the meeting will be to arrange for a person to assist with the child with autism.

Knowing that enough help is available will be reassuring to the teacher of the class and the parents of children without disabilities.

Prepare the students for the inclusion experience. Tell children, or adults, what autism is and the specific behaviors they can expect. It is important to tell them what to do to help. Be ready to answer questions.

STEP
TWO

Prepare the person with autism for the experience. Take him to the Sunday school room when there is no one there. Talk about what will happen. Show him the routine.

STEP
THREE

In addition to providing an assistant teacher, train a child to be a buddy to the new class member. In the case of an adult, prepare someone to look out for him and to make him feel secure.

STEP
FOUR

Be realistically patient. The process of forming a relationship with your new friend will take time, but the rewards will be worth it.

STEP
FIVE

Provide the teacher with this basic how-to, what-to-do, information:

- Avoid touching the child until you are aware of his response.
- Ritualistic behaviors should not be stopped unless the parents share the plan they use or that the public school teacher is using.
- Maintain as consistent a routine as possible from Sunday to Sunday.
- Allow the child to warm up to you rather than attempt to make him a part of the group. Inclusion will happen on the child's schedule. Give him time.

• Maintain the goal of being sure the child is learning at the peak of his capacity, with the ultimate goal being his becoming a part of the body of Christ.

We all like having friends who are with us just because they want to be. The person with autism and his family will be blessed by having a meaningful relationship with someone who isn't a teacher, a psychologist, or a therapist. You can be that someone—just a person who wants to be a friend and make an eternal difference in the life of someone with autism.

CHAPTER 10

ACQUIRED DISABILITIES CHANGE EXTERNAL CONDITIONS ONLY

His name is Chris. He brightens any room he enters. Chris Simpson's smile and laugh are infectious. He enjoys wearing "in" clothes, and designer sunglasses, and has been known to dye his hair. When I think of Chris, I recall one of my favorite lines from *The Sound of Music:* "How do you hold a moonbeam in your hand?" This Kentucky native exudes happiness.

My first meeting with him was through a telephone call. "Hi," he said. "My name is Chris Simpson. Everybody says I should get in touch with you."

"Why?" I asked.

"Because," he answered with great enthusiasm, "I want to minister to people who have disabilities."

That conversation started a relationship that gets better every time we talk. I don't remember when or how I learned he had a disability, but after being around him for a minute I saw how comfortable he was with his disability, his desire to minister, and his commitment to the Lord.

This bundle of personality, people lover, warm human being did not have a disability until he was sixteen. However, for a person so young he had already dealt with a lot of difficult situations: his father died, his stepfather left his mother, his mother became depressed.

I SAW HOW comfortable he was with his disability, his desire to minister, and his commitment to the Lord.

Then came January 6, 1991. On that fateful night, he was home alone in Frankfort, Kentucky. Chris thought, *With everyone gone, I need a way to protect myself.* He had always been around guns. His minister took him to target practice and drilled him on gun safety. He retrieved a .38 caliber pistol from its storage space and put two shells in it. When he stood up to return it to its place in the cupboard, the gun discharged! He still does not know what happened. He recalls the noise and the smell of gunpowder. While he knew he had been shot, he couldn't shout for help because the bullet had penetrated his right lung. The bullet entered the middle of his chest, deflected downward, severed his spinal cord, and exited through his lower back. His legs went limp. He fell to the floor. Pulling himself with his forearms, he managed to get to the phone to call 911.

An emergency team from the Frankfort fire department responded in one minute and took him to the city hospital. When the attending physicians saw the severity of his wounds, they arranged for him to be transported to the Lexington Medical Center. Fog prevented a helicopter transfer, so he was taken in an ambulance. During the twenty-minute trip, he was revived three times. Chris recalls the pain, the plastic bags over his hands to protect the evidence if his death was ruled a suicide, and thinking, *If I check out of here right now and go to God, that'll be great.*

Following seventeen hours of surgery, he slept for three days. When he regained conscious, he saw his family in vigil around his bed. Because a tube in his throat kept him from speaking, he wrote his mother three notes:

"It was an accident."

"I love you."

"It's OK." Such responses help define the kind of person Chris is.

Another part of Chris is his determination. An eight-week rehabilitation program at Cardinal Hill in Lexington took him only three. Even with all of the intervention, he knew he would never walk again. Chris remembers, "That's when I really saw God's involvement in my life for the first time. I asked myself, 'What's the big deal about not being able to walk, anyway?' And I told myself, 'Get in that wheelchair and do something!'"

And do something he did! Paralysis kept him from accepting an appointment at the Air Force Academy to study weapons design. He was accepted at the University of Kentucky to study architecture. Listening to the suggestion of some friends, Chris attended a summer program sponsored by Kentucky Christian College in Grayson. The week-long experience convinced him he wanted to go into the ministry. He didn't know what phase, maybe youth ministry.

God used several factors and situations to mold Chris's ministry.

I ASKED MYSELF, "WHAT'S THE BIG DEAL ABOUT NOT BEING ABLE TO WALK? GET IN THAT WHEELCHAIR AND DO SOMETHING!"

One factor was the more than one hundred members of his home church, Graffenburg Christian, who reached out to their young member and met his needs. He saw firsthand the easy, natural way a disability ministry should be handled.

Another factor was his work in a Christian summer camp for people with physical disabilities. He loved the work and he loved the people.

And then there was the factor of that telephone call to me in which he said, "Everybody says I should get in touch with you." He was on his way to fulfilling his desire to minister to people with disabilities.

When he graduated from Kentucky Christian College, he started working with Southeast Christian as an intern in disability ministry. He developed programs: Vacation Bible School, a respite care program, worship, crafts. He makes awareness speeches for the Christian Church Foundation for the Handicapped. In a disability awareness weekend we conducted together in Georgia, I spoke to the adults and Chris to the teenagers. My impressions of him were confirmed when a pair of teens told me, "Chris is awesome. We want him to come back."

To use Chris's words, I am glad he didn't "check out," for then I would not have known him, his love for the Lord, and his deep sense of natural, easy ministry to persons with disabilities. Knowing that the future of disability ministry in the church is, in part, in his hands is a blessing to me.

BEFRIENDING PEOPLE WITH ACQUIRED DISABILITIES

Chris's disability has not been lifelong. He is one of three groups of people with acquired disabilities who need friends.

First, there are people with traumatic brain injury.

The growing number of people with TBI is a particularly sad situation because, in many cases, their disabilities could have been prevented. The leading cause of TBI is automobile accidents in which children and adults are not properly restrained or are not wearing seat belts. Other causes, in order of frequency, are:

- motorcycle accidents
- gunshot wounds
- falls
- child abuse

The brain damage from any of these causes can range from mild to profound. The need to care for children in this category is so great that in 1990 Congress added traumatic brain injury as a separate category to IDEA.

The second group of people with acquired disabilities includes those with traumatic spinal cord injuries. The causes of TSI are similar to the causes of TBI. The difference in the two categories is that damage to the spine usually results in physical problems only, with few cognitive problems. The severity of the problem is determined by the location on the spine of the damage. From low to high, sections of the spine are called sacral, lumbar, thoracic, cervical. The higher the damaged area, the more extensive the problem. For example, a cervical level damage would be worse than a sacral.

ENCOURAGE him to join a support group to hear how someone else has dealt or is dealing with the situation.

The third category of people with acquired disabilities is widely known—those who have had strokes. The medical term is "cerebrovascular accident." The CVA is created by a lack of blood flow to the brain. Blood clots, hardening of the arteries by plaque formation, and high blood pressure are common causes.

After a stroke, the person may have difficulty talking or walking. Wheelchairs, canes, and walkers are often used. The need for therapy and medical intervention is routine. The need for friendship is always what the doctor ordered.

In order to help a friend who has lived a life without restrictions and suddenly becomes dependent on others, you need to show great empathy. Wear his shoes for a day. How would you adjust to not driving a car, not being able to communicate clearly, not being capable of taking care of your daily life functions? A look at the following information will make empathy easier.

Let's start with a two-prong language situation. On the one hand, you will hear and learn new words.

- "Quadriplegia" means paralysis has affected all four limbs.
- "Paraplegia" means paralysis of the lower half of the body
- "Hemiplegia" means total or partial paralysis of one side of the body
- "Aphasia" refers to partial or full loss of the power to use or comprehend words.

Listen for new words and keep a good dictionary handy. Knowing what is being communicated will assist in developing friendship.

On the other hand, while you will want to be sensitive to your friend's new vocabulary, don't hesitate to say, "walk" and "run." To the person in a wheelchair say, "Do you want to take a walk?" not "Do you want to take a roll?" Don't use words like, "cripple," "lame," "deformed."

Your friend's mobility will change. More than likely he will be in a wheelchair, need crutches, or wear a brace. These devices are a part of the person and should be treated that way. Never call attention to them, unless it is easy and natural. For example, asking, "Do you have a new chair?" would be appropriate. But to say, "I bet that chair helps you get around better," is obvious and strained.

Sharing his debilitating experience with others who understand will be helpful to your friend. Encourage him to join a support group. There will be much for him to learn about his new lifestyle. Hearing how someone else has dealt or is dealing with the situation will help your friend cope and adjust. The social services department in the hospital or rehabilitation center probably will suggest a support group as part of your friend's discharge plan. If so, find out where and when the group meets and what you can do to help your friend get there. Look also for parent-to-parent groups.

> CAREFUL *listening will help you understand what your friend is saying. Be honest; don't say you understand if you don't.*

To find a support group, consider these sources:
- Community churches
- Therapists, case managers, social workers and doctors
- Your school district's special education department
- Your local ARC (Association for Retarded Citizens) and MHMR (Mental Health and Mental Retardation) offices, which sponsor support groups for parents of children and adults with special needs.
- *Exceptional Parent* magazine and NATHHAN (National Challenged Homeschoolers Associated Network) connects parents who have children with similar disabilities. Find Exceptional Parent on the Internet at http://www.eparent.com, or call 800-562-1973. E-mail NATHHAN at: nathanews@aol.com or call 253-857-4257.

Your friend probably will have problems with his speech. Careful listening will help you understand what your friend is saying. Be honest; don't say you understand if you don't. If a language board is being used, learn how to operate it and help your friend use it. If handwriting is the only option, write it.

If the person has been physically active, and when the doctor clears him to do so, encourage him to swim, join a wheelchair basketball team, or otherwise be active. Check in your community or region for organizations that can help. Maybe your church could sponsor a team.

It is important that the person's friends do not desert him. Your role can be to help keep a strong support system available. When a friend of mine had a stroke, I called his hospital's social worker to ask what I could do to help. Her advice is still valid: "Continue to do what you have always done with him." In a few days I went by for lunch with him. Even though I had to learn his new speech and language patterns, our friendship continued.

YOUR FRIEND'S *condition need not be the focal point of the conversation, but know that he is constantly aware of it.*

If your friend's condition is so severe he remains at home, visit often, encourage others to visit, have card showers at birthdays and holidays. When you visit, narrate. Be cautious about asking questions, especially if the person has difficulty expressing himself. Talk about the ride over, the weather, what is happening in town, etc. Be natural. Talk about all facets of your own life, the good and the bad. Trying to avoid negatives will create awkwardness. Your friend's condition need not be the focal point of the conversation, but know that he is constantly aware of it. I learned this lesson from a dear friend with cancer. When I visited her house one afternoon, she was playing bridge with three friends. She told me that she had ignored my advice about an investment she had made and had "lost her blouse." I remarked, "The cancer has gone to your brain." One player gasped. Mary touched her arm and said, "You have known for six months that I have cancer and have never mentioned it. It is a part of me. I don't mind talking about it. I think about it all the time." Whatever direction your conversations take, you will learn that just being there is the best therapy.

If you are uncomfortable with the protocol of relating to a friend with an acquired disability, let your friend teach you as you go. The first time Chris and I went out to eat together I learned a valuable lesson about how to help with his wheelchair. We went to a Mexican restaurant near my office. I parked in the marked space by the curb cut, got the wheels to Chris's chair out of the trunk, helped him put the chair together, got Chris in the chair, and left to park my car in the lot. The food was great and the conversation better. Afterward, when we went outside, I said, "You wait here, Chris. I'll go get the car."

Chris answered, "Oh, that's OK, Jim. I prefer to go with you." He wanted to walk with his friend to the car. At the car, he transferred himself from his chair to the front seat and we put the dismantled chair in the trunk and back seat. That is the way friends would do it.

Relax. Being a friend to a person with a spinal cord injury, a traumatic brain injury, or a stroke is easy, especially if you have a teacher like Chris. Be a force in helping your friend return to the peak of his ability. Although his role in his community will change, he remains a valuable person who can contribute to his family, his community, and his church. A faithful friend will fill the bill!

CHAPTER 11

ASSISTING THE FAMILY
DEALING WITH DISABILITY

Her name is Dee. Her maternal grandfather probably would say, "Deedra Kay," but she has always been Dee to me. I knew about her before I met her. The word was that she was having problems with her bone growth. As her mother, Judy Mentzer, described the situation, "From the beginning Deedra was unhappy and obviously in pain, but the pediatrician could not find an apparent cause for her discomfort, and his only suggestion was to change her formula. On Sunday morning, December 7, 1975, after a particularly difficult week, I took her to the emergency room, where it was discovered that both bones of her left leg were broken. The radiologist said that the fractures were old and probably occurred before, but possibly at birth (September 9, 1975). While putting on her first cast, the orthopedist noticed a brown spot on her stomach and upon examination found several more. Called "cafe-au-lait spots," they are symptoms of neurofibromatosis, a disease that causes fibromas (tumors) to grow in the nerves throughout the body. That was Dee's problem. A tumor was growing on the nerve in the long bone of her leg, causing the bone to break and forcing it apart until there was a small section with no bone, forming a pseudo-arthrosis (false joint).

Dee's parents had been students of mine, and her maternal grandparents, Jean and Russell Morgan, and I were members of the same college staff. However, it was not until Drew, her father, became the minister of a church in Knoxville that my relationship with Dee began. Before I tell you that part of the story, I want Judy to explain more about her medical condition:

"Because of our concern for Dee's leg, it was easy to forget about all the other problems that neurofibromatosis can cause. But forgetting them did not keep them from occurring. The week of Thanksgiving, 1978, when she was three, we noticed that her eyes were crossing. It was December 14 before I could get an appointment with an ophthalmologist. He examined her and had her admitted to the hospital for tests. In that short time Dee lost all of her vision in the right eye and could see only light, large shapes, and some colors in her left eye. The CT scans revealed bilateral optic gliomas (large tumors in both optic nerves). The tumors were growing toward her eyeballs causing them to protrude. In January, 1979, Dee had five weeks of radiation to stop the growth and shrink the tumors. The treatment was successful, but nothing could be done to restore her sight."

Dee has had many surgeries. In spite of all her problems, Dee is a ray of sunshine.

It was Dee's blindness that brought me in closer contact with her. When I directed the Children's Rehabilitation Center in Knoxville, we offered a joint program with the Knox County School System for young children who were blind. Dubbed VITAL (Visually Impaired Training and Learning), the goal of the program was to give preschool blind children a head start. Dee was enrolled. I have two wonderful memories of her from those days.

Dee often had something to report. One day an assistant in the class was having trouble understanding what Dee was trying to tell her. The part of the message the assistant understood was that Dee had something to tell me. When I went to the therapy room, the aid was asking, "What do you want to tell Mr. Pierson?"

Dee responded with a sentence that ended with something that sounded like, "God's will."

Thinking the sentence had something to do with Dee's blindness as it related to God's will, the aid reassured Dee that she was a wonderful person and God loved her. Just looking at Dee's face, it was obvious that was not the correct interpretation.

Using the interpretation techniques outlined for you on page sixty-two, I realized we needed the subject of Dee's report. I asked, "Who did it for you?"

Her faced brightened and she indicated it was her maternal grandfather. I knew he was closely involved with her life. Remembering an earlier conversation with her mother about something he had done for Dee, I asked, "Wasn't it nice that your grandfather put guardrails on your bed so you won't roll out?"

Dee beamed and we went on to another subject. The aid smiled sheepishly and said, "How did you figure it out?" I had to confess that I did not have superior interpretation skills nor was I a solver of riddles. In my conversation with Judy, Dee's mother, I had learned that Judy's parents had been to visit and that her father had put guardrails on Dee's bed. "Guardrails" and "God's will" have a similar ring if not articulated clearly.

The second event happened to a group of visitors. The University of Tennessee cheerleaders had brought Smoky Dog, the huge, stuffed mascot of the football team, for the children in the program to

DEE IS A WONDERFUL READER. SHE HAS READ HER BRAILLE BIBLE THROUGH TWO TIMES, PLUS MANY OTHER BOOKS.

enjoy. The members of the squad were having a heart-wrenching experience watching the youngsters explore their environment using touch. Dee walked over to the soft, furry toy and "studied" it with her fingers. At this point, Dee was losing her vision but still had some color perception, especially of large objects. Taking advantage of an opportunity to encourage Dee to use her residual vision, the teacher asked, "What color is it, Dee?"

She rubbed the dog for a few seconds and answered, "I fink it is brue." She was correct. Several Kleenex were used.

A favorite Mentzer family story has to do with a Christmas gift. An aunt had given Dee a Cabbage Patch doll. When Dee opened the package she studied the doll's face with her fingers. Then she asked, "Is this doll ugly?"

In spite of all of her problems, Dee is a ray of sunshine. She has had many surgeries. One procedure involved having ten of her teeth removed because her mouth was too small for them. The rods in her leg would often slip and start infections, which meant more surgeries and more hospital time. Her mother, who has always been by her side, describes her daughter as "a loving, happy, cheerful person and a joy to all who know her. She has a beautiful smile and a wonderful sense of humor and finds funny things around her every day. She is a wonderful reader and has read her braille Bible through two times, plus many other books."

Her mother's comment about Dee's reading reminds me of another story. She invited me to come to her house one Sunday afternoon so she could read braille for me. When she finished, I told her, "You are good."

"I ought to be good. It took me seven years to learn to do it!" she responded with a typical "Deeism."

Dee is involved in living. Her mom, or should I say, transportation coordinator, explains:

"She loves country music, talking on the phone with her friends, singing, and celebrating birthdays—especially her own! She has taken swimming lessons for nine years, goes horseback riding, has participated in several statewide horse shows, and takes piano lessons."

> DEE'S MOM says Dee "loves country music, talking on the phone with her friends, singing, and celebrating birthdays— especially her own!

When she was in the ninth grade, Dee became a student at the Tennessee School for the Blind. The choices were for her to stay in her local school system or to go to TSB. I remember the difficulty Drew and Judy had making the decision. Perhaps a significant factor in the decision was her brother Doug's opinion. Having observed his fellow students poking fun, teasing, or otherwise being unkind to another mainstreamed blind student in his school, he didn't want his sister to be subjected to the same treatment.

While it would be difficult to be away from Dee, the family determined that, for her own safety and emotional well-being, she would do better getting training at the respected state facility. Judy tells of the commitment she and Drew made to Dee: "She began attending TSB in the fall of 1989 and stayed there for five years. We promised her that if she went away to school she could come home every weekend. The first four years the students were bused home every three to five weeks, and we went after her the other weeks. We estimate that we made 224 round-trips to Nashville those first four years. The fifth year she was bused home every week. Dee graduated from TSB on June 2, 1995, with a Special Education Certificate."

Commitment, devotion, concern, love, availability are only a few of the adjectives that describe Dee's family. An example was the family's attendance at her graduation from Tennessee School for the Blind. I went to that June 2 graduation—along with her mother and dad and brother Doug, and her aunts, grandparents, uncles, and cousins. Some had driven great distances. In their tradition, they were all where they needed to be—with Dee, celebrating her victory.

> WHEN YOU *befriend a person with a disability, he or she will have family also in need of support. The toll is heavy on marriages experiencing disability.*

There were thirteen graduates that year. Each one walked down the aisle and took a seat. Like her fellow graduates, Dee did it without an attendant.

The Tennessee Commissioner of Education who gave the commencement address was moved by the processional of the graduates into the auditorium. She remarked, "I want to congratulate each of you. You have accomplished a lot. Your teachers have assisted you in becoming independent. You have demonstrated your accomplishments for us today by entering and finding your seats without any help. You have reached many goals." It was a thrilling moment.

Dee now lives in Illinois where her father took another church. I enjoy calling her on her private line and having my letters to her brailled. She likes that touch. You can do the same thing for your friend by contacting a local organization serving people who are blind and asking them how you may find a braillist. The service of brailling your letter may be performed without cost.

Before Dee and her parents moved to Illinois, my wife and I took them and her maternal grandmother to a Chinese restaurant (Dee's favorite food) for lunch. After meeting at my office, we decided to drive two cars to the restaurant. Dee and I rode together. She talked all the way. When we arrived, I practiced my best blind etiquette. She took my elbow and as we approached a curb, I stopped. She said, "You're good!"

Dee is an inspiration. She brightens her world with love and happiness.

HELPING THE FAMILY

When you befriend a person with a disability, he or she will have family also in need of support. The toll is heavy on marriages experiencing disability; four out of five end in divorce. People often pull away from families of children with disabilities because, they report, "We don't know what to say or do." Perhaps, too, we think we don't know how to help with the feelings they are experiencing. Leave that role to the professionals. You be a friend.

Drew Mentzer, Dee's father, was the featured speaker for a disability awareness program at Johnson Bible College. His speech was a double blessing to me. First, I was proud of my former public speaking student, and second, I received excellent ideas for what to suggest to people who want to help families.

He based his comments on the different feelings of Peter's family when Peter was released from prison, compared with those of James's family when Herod put James to death (Acts 12:1-17). Peter's family was having a party; James's family was having a funeral. Drew's analogy was clear; Peter's family would be the one who does not have a child with a disability and James's family would be the one with a child with a disability. Drew's bright mind and sensitive heart are in these suggestions. Use them in your friendship with a family experiencing disability.

- Be a servant to the family. Take up the towel and basin. Do not see yourself as superior. The family needs friends who will serve.
- See life from their perspective. Learn their vocabulary. Know the world of dealing with a child with a disability.
- Encourage the family. They know pain, fear, worry, and grief. Help them know compassion, joy, and hope.
- Be sensitive. Don't thank God for your healthy child if your gratitude is based on comparison with their child. Parents of children with disabilities are thankful for them too. God made us all.
- Don't assign blame or ask if they know what they did to cause the problem. Parents suffer from insensitive questions. Drew was once asked, "Was it something you did or was it Satan's doing?" God is in charge and does all things according to His purpose and plan for us.
- You don't have to be able to provide answers, but be ready to help the family learn good lessons.
- Guide families to know that it is all right to ask for help.
- Cheer the family on to victory. Be there in the good times and the bad.
- "Minister to both families," were Drew's exact words. I was struck by them. A minister by profession, this father of a daughter with a disability

was unselfishly reminding us that both families need to receive and give ministry. Drew's comment suggests that, first, we need to minister to families without disabilities as well as to those with. Second, the family dealing with the disability needs to reach out and minister to others in spite of their pain.

- Include the family in the life of the congregation. Make it easy for the parents to attend church functions. If their Bible school class is having a party, volunteer to sit with the child.

HURTFUL WORDS, HEALING WORDS

In my experience of working with parents of children with disabilities, I have heard consistent reports about the insensitive, unkind statements people make to them. They range from, "What do you think God is punishing you for?" to, "God knew what He was doing when He selected a strong person like you to have a child like this."

Learn words that will encourage. These examples will help you phrase sentences that will encourage:

"I have learned so much from you as I've watched you handle your child."

"You are the expert on the needs of your child."

"Take care of yourself."

"I see a lot of love in you."

"It is not your fault."

Knowing that there are four times of universal concern for the family will enable you to know *especially* when to be a friend. First, when the diagnosis is made; second, when the child starts to school; third, when the child is finished with school; fourth, when the parents realize they can no longer provide care for their child.

A congregation can be a real resource for the family. The family's number-one need is respite care.

Simply stated, they need some time away, some extra hands occasionally, and someone to do the chores when time gets tight. Putting yourself in the family's place will allow you to add chores to this list that will make their days easier.

- provide transportation
- shop for groceries
- care for the lawn
- do the laundry
- write letters
- baby-sit

Providing Sunday school and worship experiences for the child will serve the family. Christian parents want their child to develop faith, become a Christian, have church friends, and grow spiritually.

Siblings of the child with a disability also need attention. While the reaction varies, some siblings will overachieve to make up for the child with the disability, some will resent the time the parents spend with the child with a disability, some will be fine and choose a special education or helping profession, some will be embarrassed, and some will be jealous of the child. Whatever the case, a little attention from a friend will be a great benefit.

Your friend's family will be better off because you care. Find out what they need by being close enough to notice. Follow Drew's advice: "Cheer them on to victory. Be there in the good times and the bad."

CHAPTER 12

REHABILITATING THE WHOLE PERSON

His name is Evan. He is one of my newest friends. He doesn't walk. He doesn't talk. I have never worked with him. His mother provided me with most of the information I have. However, I was involved in one of the most important, if not the most important, events in his life: his baptism. Before we hear that story, let's talk about Evan.

When Evan Farris was born on August 16, 1977, he sustained brain damage. As he developed, his condition worsened. At the age of one, he had surgery to correct a vision problem. He was healthy, but his physical problems were obvious. He couldn't sit alone until he was six. He didn't walk until he was nine, and then only with assistance. He couldn't speak. In addition to a tonsillectomy and ear tubes, he had two major surgeries on his legs. His mental retardation was at first rated mild and then changed to severe. At fifteen he started having seizures. They are now controlled by medication.

When I met him at nineteen years of age, he could no longer walk and used a wheelchair. Communication was made possible by a computer with software programmed to respond to a touch window, which in turn produces synthetic speech.

This young man's story could not be told without talking about his family's role in it. Early in his life, his mother educated children about disability by using her son. Peggy relates an event:

> In the grocery store one day a little boy came up to me and asked, "What's wrong with him? Why are you pushing him in a baby carriage? He's too big."
>
> As I was about to answer the questions, an embarrassed mother grabbed his arm, whisked him away and said, "Just don't look at him. I'll explain it later."
>
> I could have let it go, but I didn't. I ran down the aisle pushing Evan and cornered this mother and child. I got down on eye level to the child and answered his questions. I told him that Evan's brain was sick and it couldn't tell his legs to get out of that chair and walk. He laughed when I agreed it looked silly to see such a big boy being pushed in a baby carriage. I told him that Evan had a beautiful smile and that if he smiled, Evan would give it back to him. He did and sure enough Evan gave him a glorious smile. Satisfied, the child waved good-bye to Evan. With tears running down her face, his mother thanked me.

Peggy often took Evan to his brother's school. The students were urged to touch him and not be afraid, and to ask questions. Evan relished the attention he received from his brother's classmates. The students were giving him positive attention. Their touches, smiles, and words were sincere. Under Peggy's sensitive tutelage, Evan was providing excellent disability awareness training for his brother's friends.

As a student, Evan made his world better. He received the principal's Humanitarian Award from his middle school along with his peer tutor, Stephanie. The citation, in part, stated:

> This year the award must be given to two very special students: Stephanie Prince and Evan Farris. Without Evan, Stephanie would not have had the rare opportunity to give to and care for another human being, an experience that reaches far beyond the realm and scope of most young people her age. Without Stephanie, Evan would have missed the unsolicited love and nurturing that sometimes can come only from one's peer. What a team these two have become. Evan has given so much, and Stephanie has received so much—Stephanie has given so much, and Evan has received so much. If a principal's humanitarian award is to be presented, it must be presented to both of these courageous students. Together they are the whole picture.

It is important to know that Stephanie, the peer tutor, is in college preparing to be a special educator. She is one of two students whose association with Evan has influenced them to make special education a vocation.

As a young adult, Evan's education is preparing him for the future. He is taking classes in home living skills, and he works in a JC Penney stock room two times a week with a one-on-one job coach. One day a week he shops for groceries, eats in a restaurant, and goes to the mall.

Attending church has always been a part of Evan's life. Early on he often stayed in the nursery. As he got older, a big person in a big wheelchair in a small classroom with small children became a problem from time to time. The children were told that Evan was an assistant to the teacher. Peggy returned to her role as her son's advocate, as she helped teachers and students understand her son's condition and his importance as a person.

The goal Peggy and Milton have always had for their son is that he be involved in the real world, with real people. Therefore, when it came time to think about his future residential placement, the Farrises became advocates for group home living. They reasoned, since Evan had always lived at home, why should he now live in an institution? They worked to develop a group home service in their community. When Evan finishes school, he will make the transition to a group home with two or three other people, plus house managers.

Being Christians, his parents were also concerned about his eternal home. On that note, let's talk about the first time I met Evan.

On a beautiful autumn Sunday, I was at the Northside Christian Church in Marietta, Georgia, to participate in a disability awareness program. Following my sermon, I sat on the front pew. When the invitation was offered, I heard a wheelchair squeak and turned to see who was coming. Evan was being pushed down the aisle by his parents. For some time he had been talking on

COMMUNICATION FOR EVAN IS MADE POSSIBLE BY A COMPUTER THAT PRODUCES SYNTHETIC SPEECH.

his language board about becoming a Christian. He
had decided that this day would be a good day to do
it. What followed was a moving scene. Jack Ballard,
the minister, a longtime friend of the family and
mine, explained that because of Evan's lack of
speech, the taking of his confession would be different. But when he asked Evan if he believed Jesus was
God's Son, Evan's face beamed. The look on his face
spoke pages.

He was baptized later, with family and friends present. I will always be grateful that I was one of them.
The minister, placing his body close to Evan's, said,
"Evan, I am going to hold you as close as possible
and lower myself into the water with you. As the
water surrounds your body, you will know you are
surrounded by the love of God, the love of your family, and the love of your preacher. I baptize you into
the name of Jesus Christ." It was a happy day.

While Peggy was picking up her dry cleaning one
day, the clerk told Peggy that she had named her son
Evan as well, and the name means "Gift from God."
Evan *is* a gift from God, and Peggy refers to him as
such. He has a soul, a soul that will be returned to
its creator. The role of a friend is to see that every
gift from God is taught, and given an opportunity to
express his faith.

THE REHABILITATION
OF THE SOUL IN A FLAWED BODY

Evan's baptism raises questions in people's minds.
Does he understand what has transpired? Wouldn't
God understand if he were never baptized? How was
he taught about faith?

The question of how much comprehension takes
place is easy to answer. The people who will have the
most trouble understanding faith are those with
mental retardation, but of this group, 85 percent can

be taught the facts about faith. You do not need to worry about how much they understand. Your role is to get your friend into a Christian education program where the learning can take place.

Will God understand if a person is never baptized? In cases where the person's level of function is so low that he simply cannot comprehend basic facts, the answer is "yes." In those situations, the person is surrounded by God's love and mercy. But in situations where the mental age is sufficient to learn, the person should be taught.

Evan was taught the same way anyone learns: by exposure to the truth. The teaching has to be done with more simplicity and more repetition. The teaching must be consistent and be practically applied to the person's daily experience. Then the newborn faith has to be maintained and developed in a caring environment of a loving congregation. Teaching God's truth should be a part of the rehabilitation plan of every person with a disability.

LOOK PAST THE LIMITATIONS

Over the years, I have observed many professionals whose work has made a difference in the lives of people with disabilities. The changes have been amazing. An occupational therapist designs a switch that allows a young wheelchair user to control his chair with his breath. He has freedom. The family had been told that their child might not walk. A physical therapist saw the possibilities. After months of therapy, the child walked.

Acquiring speech, learning to walk, and developing social skills are important. Evan was given the best in educational, medical, and therapeutic care. His family wanted him to have the finest in spiritual therapy as well. Knowing God provides hope. Isaiah predicts, "Your God will come, . . . he will come to save you. Then will the eyes of the blind be opened and the ears of the deaf unstopped. Then will the lame leap like a deer, and the mute tongue shout for joy" (Isaiah 35:4-6, *New International Version*). I want that promise for my friends with disabilities.

The rehabilitation of the whole person is important. All parents want their children to achieve. This desire is just as strong for parents of children with disabilities. Two situations in my experience illustrate this fact. I call this "The Tale of Two Mothers."

> "**H**E IS *coming to save you. . . . Those who could not speak will shout and sing!*"

When I was a practicing speech pathologist, I worked with a little girl named Laurie Muller, who had a rare neurological disorder. She was hospitalized often. Her parents loved her and wanted her to function at the peak of her capacity. I had worked with her for weeks with no results. Finally, I put her in a group of three other children who were just beginning to develop speech sounds. Using animal sounds, the stimulation work began. The other three children made good progress. Laurie didn't. She was only hearing what the other children said. Then, one day I held up the picture of a sheep and asked, "What sound does the sheep make?"

Child one answered, "Baa, baa."

Child two, "Baa, baa."

Child three, "Baa, baa."

And then Laurie said, "Baa, baa."

I thought, *I will strike while the iron is hot.*

I said, "Baa, baa, baa."

She said, "Baa, baa, baa."

I said, "Mama."

She said, "Mama."

When it was time for Laurie to be picked up by her mother, I took her to the waiting room. When her mother arrived, I said, "Who is that?"

She responded, "Mama."

A delighted, weeping mother reported, "I have waited five years to hear her say that."

The other mother wanted her son to have the best residential care. Mark, her son, was nineteen years old. His problems were severe. He had no speech, but he could walk—and walk fast! Safety was his mother's major concern for him. Reluctantly, she placed him in special facilities. Staff members had difficulty keeping him away from things that could harm him. One day he noticed the device on the washing machine that regulates the amount of liquid detergent per load of clothes. Because he was learning to suck, he was attracted to the tube of the apparatus. He yanked it loose and sucked from the exposed end. The swallowed detergent badly burned his esophagus, and he had to have regular surgeries to keep it open. On the last trip for the surgery, the routine changed. Something else was wrong. The physician found an advanced brain tumor. Like Mark, the tumor moved quickly; he died within hours. My wife and I went to the funeral. His mother had written a tribute to her son. She said, in part, "At night, in my dreams, Mark could always talk, and we would have long conversations. My dreams were very real, but then I would wake up to discover again that the conversation was just a dream. Isaiah 35:4-6 became Mark's Scripture that I held for him: 'He is coming to save you. . . . Those who could not speak will shout and sing!'" *(The Living Bible).*

HAVING AN understanding of Heaven is important for the person with disability. Persons with mental retardation are keenly aware of eternal matters.

Both mothers wanted the best for their children. Both mothers were pleased with their children's achievements. Both achieved goals that were important. But one goal is eternal.

Having an understanding of Heaven is important for the person with disability. Persons with mental retardation are keenly aware of eternal matters. Sheryl, who lived at Riverwood Christian Community for two years before her death, had Down syndrome and a heart defect that caused a circulation problem resulting in discolored lips and fingers. At Sheryl's funeral service, Paula, a fellow resident, gave an eulogy. I was amazed at her insights about what was important. Paula recalled, "I remember the day Sheryl moved to our home. She was so excited she wouldn't quit talking. She went to work. She cried when she got her first paycheck. As each day passed, she was more and more independent. Sometimes she got a little too independent and the staff had to help her along. We loved Sheryl very much and will miss her. I know she is with the Lord and she is now a perfect person. She is in Heaven now, walking on streets of gold. She has no purple lips, no purple fingers, and no more Down syndrome."

Special education, speech pathology, physical therapy, occupational therapy, psychology, and other helping professions are important to the development of the mind, the speech, and the limbs. Christian education is important to the development of the soul. It can start with a friend who cares, who teaches truth, and who models faith.

CONCLUSION

MY NAME IS JIM

My name is Jim. In working with people with disabilities, I have served in many roles over the years: speech therapist, administrator of a children's rehabilitation center, consultant in disability ministry, Sunday school teacher, college teacher of special education, seminar leader, and developer of group homes. My favorite role is friend.

When the inclusion concept first appeared, I thought it was a great idea. Reality struck, however, as we discovered that sometimes inclusion works and sometimes it doesn't. The sure way to achieve inclusion is to leave it to friendship: two people mutually helping, gaining from each other. In my roles as a professional and as friend I have received more than I have given. Three lessons learned from three friends with disabilities will illustrate my point.

LESSON ONE

Just being with a friend is blessing enough. I learned that from Rachel, who has Down syndrome. A Virginian, she lives with her parents, a brother and a sister, and lots of pets. From our first meeting we liked each other. Once when I stayed at their house, Rachel was given the responsibility of being my hostess. Upon my arrival, she guided me to my room, showed me where the light switches were, showed me how to open the closet door, and gave several other directives. We crossed the hall to the bathroom. She pointed out my towels, my soap, and the toothpaste. Then she showed me the commode and added a reminder, "Don't forget to flush!"

When her family attends church conventions, we eat together. Rachel and I sit together in the restaurant. She likes lettuce. Once I was speaking in Hampton, Virginia, which is next door to her town, Newport News. Her family attended most of the services. The other members of her family sat together, but Rachel sat with me on the front row. She was happy to sit quietly with her friend. Being together was the most important factor.

LESSON TWO

Greg taught me that ability doesn't influence true success, mission, or purpose. He said (through his brother's voice) in a biographical filmstrip, "I have cerebral palsy due to the lack of oxygen at birth. Some people think that being handicapped is such a waste. They feel sorry for us thinking we can't do anything. I have never been able to walk and it is not easy for me to talk. Many things I can't do, but I love God and want to serve Him. I've found joy in Christ and He has made my life useful, I hope, to Him and to others."

Not all ministers have to attend a seminary to be effective.

Greg has prepared sermons that were projected on a screen in the church, he has written books of poetry, he writes letters to cheer people, and he sends cards (typed on his typewriter, which takes a long time). To those who know him he is an inspiration.

Greg is working! He is the greeter at a Builders Square store in Ohio. He is still in his wheelchair, his speech is still unintelligible, but three days a week he works. His beautiful smile is augmented by a synthetic voice produced by a DynaVox. To communicate, Greg touches a key that triggers a prerecorded message: "Housewares are on aisle four." "Have a good day." "Seniors get a 20 percent discount on Wednesday."

SOMEDAY, *in Christ, the person will be whole. The soul is more important than the body.*

David Wecker, a columnist with the *Cincinnati Post,* wrote a great article about Greg's job (October 17, 1996, p. B1). He told the story of a shopper who needed assistance finding a plumber's helper. Greg pushed the pad that announces that plumbing supplies are on aisle six. The shopper found his merchandise. Mr. Wecker reported, "Greg struggled to express a thought that wasn't in his DynaVox sound bite data bank. I had to ask him to repeat it for me three times. Finally, I got it."

"God has me here for a reason," says Greg. "It's slow. But God goes at His own pace."

LESSON THREE

Not all ministers have to attend a seminary to be effective. Lee is a friendly, good-looking man with mental retardation, who lives at Riverwood Christian Community. In spite of rapid speech, poor syntax, and poor articulation, he communicates clearly. Once, when my wife and I were at Riverwood for a party that we sponsor every year, we told the residents that my mother was not well. The residents already knew that my sisters and I were arranging to place our parents in an assisted living program. While I enjoyed the party, my heart was heavy. I needed a minister.

After the party, Lee and I took the trash to the

dump site. He was uncommonly quiet. After a bit he said, "You me buddy. Me sad about you mom. Me pray real loud before me go to bed and at Sunday school. Jesus make her better. I ask God not let you heart hurt." My eyes moistened. My heart smiled. He ministered to me. He met my needs. A few months later when I drove my parents from the house they had lived in for sixty-three years, I remembered my minister's prayer, "I ask God not let you heart hurt."

While I have learned many lessons about life from my friends with disabilities, I have also learned what is most important: someday, in Christ, the person will be whole. The soul is more important than the body. Judy Mentzer, Dee's mother, reminded me of this fact: "When Dee was ten she was baptized. Even with her limited abilities she knew that this is what the Lord wanted her to do. There are many things that she will never comprehend but she knows without any doubt that one day she will be in Heaven, free from casts and braces and canes, free from pain and the problems that she has experienced here. She knows that she will see Jesus and all the wonders that He has prepared for those who love and serve Him.

JIM PIERSON KNOWS THAT FRIENDSHIPS WITH RESIDENTS LIKE BRIAN COLMER BLOOM EASILY AT RIVERWOOD.

"Not long ago I found a poem with a verse that applied to Dee:

 I asked God to heal my handicapped child
 But God said, 'No.'
 He said, 'Her spirit is beautiful and her body is
  only temporary.'"

Thank you, Rachel, Greg, Lee, Dee, and Judy, and all my other friends who have taught me so much. Thank you, Sean, for reminding your grandfather that the way to build a friendship with a person with a disability is to respond to him or her, not the disability. Making the person a part of my community, my life, and my church will lead to natural inclusion. The results will be a mutually beneficial relationship with eternal consequences. The process starts by asking, "What is your name?"

THE LITTLE BOY WHO INSPIRES MY COMMITMENT TO MINISTRY

His name is David. His friendship is special to me. First, he is a delightful young man. Second, he brings renewal to my ministry with people with disabilities. With the arrival of my sixtieth year, I am reinspired by my eight-year-old friend.

His parents named him David for two reasons. First, they wanted a simple, easy-to-say name. Second, they wanted him, like David of the Bible, to be able to slay all of the giants in his life. From the first time I met David Delafield of Louisville, Kentucky, I determined that I was going to help this young man with Down syndrome kill his giants.

My introduction to David occurred while I was working in a disability awareness program that his mother had organized in their home congregation, Southeast Christian Church. I noticed his natty church attire, especially his necktie. For a four year old, he looked very comfortable. The reason? He wanted to be like his father. When his dad wore a tie, David wore one as well.

As the weekend went on, it was clear that a special bond had developed between us. The meaning of our bond became apparent as we went to Sunday lunch.

David and his family and my wife and I were having lunch in a Louisville restaurant. After we parked our car, I walked to his car and offered to carry him. Immediately he came to me (not a frequent response according to his parents). When I carried him into the dining room, I noticed the all-too-typical reactions—people staring, talking behind their hands, and diverting their eyes when caught staring. Sometimes in similar situations, I have talked to the people who were staring, explained the disability, and generally became an instant advocate for the person. With David, I didn't do anything overtly. I felt sad that he would have to deal with such unkindness and wished I could always be available to run interference for this precious little boy. Knowing that would not be possible, I renewed my commitment to being a friend to people with disabilities by helping others to see they have value, their feelings are important, and they have souls. David's mom echoes my feelings, "My love for David is not based on his 'normalness' but instead on his inherent worth as a human being created in God's image."

> "MY LOVE FOR David is not based on his 'normalness' but instead on his inherent worth as a human created in God's image."

That weekend started a wonderful friendship with his family. His dad, Don, is the head of their church's counseling service. His mom, Danna, is a counselor in a private practice. His sister, Jessica, fourteen months older than David, adores her brother, likes mint chocolates, and enjoys stuffed animals.

A nice part of our friendship is participating in disability awareness programs together. Usually I speak and Danna sings the poignant song, "Sometimes Miracles Hide." The lyrics describe a couple who decide not to abort a child with a disability. Near the end of the solo, David joins his mother on the stage and sometimes sings along.

When the four Delafields came to our house for a weekend, David showed us how comfortable he is with us. Because they arrived past David and Jessica's bedtime, their parents quickly put them into their nightclothes. Thinking that his parents were leaving them with us, David walked over to his parents and said, "Go!" He was ready for them to leave. He wanted to get on with the evening with his new friends.

David is aware of serious matters. When his paternal grandfather died, David showed a remarkable understanding of death. Don and Danna had prepared him by explaining that his grandfather was sick and would soon go to Heaven and live with Jesus.

When it was obvious the end was near, David and Danna were on the way to grandfather's house. The call came on the car phone that Danna's father had died. Realizing that the funeral

HIS PARENTS NAMED HIM DAVID, BECAUSE THEY WANTED HIM, LIKE DAVID OF THE BIBLE, TO BE ABLE TO SLAY ALL OF THE GIANTS IN HIS LIFE

home had not had time to remove the body, Danna was concerned. Would it be good for David to see his grandfather's body in his bed?

Her concerns were short-lived. David walked into the bedroom, saw his grandfather, started to approach for his customary hug but stopped and asked, "Dead?" His mother nodded. David responded, "Jesus Christ. Home."

Respond to *David and each individual like him as a person, not as a person with a diagnosis.*

My friendship with David reached a crescendo in Kansas City at the North American Christian Convention in 1997. This was the event that brought my recommitment to my ministry. I addressed a main session on the subject of compassion. Before my message, Danna sang "Sometimes Miracles Hide" and, in regular fashion, David joined her.

During the preparation of the sermon, I thought it would be effective to have a person with a disability as a part of the concluding illustration. Since David would be there, he would be ideal. While I wanted it to be a good experience for him, I recognized it was a lot for a little fellow to handle.

With the approval of his parents and their assuring comment, "When he sees you, he will be fine," we agreed that David would join me on the platform. Using the story of the Good Samaritan, I underscored the necessity of responding to the needs of one person at a time. To illustrate, I reviewed various statistics about needy groups and told a story from my experience. For example, I reported the thousands of children who are hungry and related the story of a little girl whose breakfast I bought.

When I talked about the needs of the disability community, David walked onto the stage. I picked him up and urged the audience to respond to David and each individual like him as a person, not as a person with a diagnosis.

David's intent gaze into my eyes let me know it was a good experience for him. For me, the moment was a catalyst for my recommitment to my ministry.

The opportunity to encourage thousands of convention goers to treat people like David with Christ-like love was a giant step in my personal pledge to run interference for David and people like him. I pray that many of the people who heard that sermon and who read this book will open their hearts, lives, and churches to people with disabilities. I pray also that the information in this book will motivate you to make the commitment to help slay the giants in the life of one person with a disability.